ART OF
DRUM LAYERING

Eddie Bazil

PC Publishing

PC Publishing
Keeper's House
Merton
Thetford
Norfolk IP25 6QH
UK

Tel +44 (0)1953 889900
email info@pc-publishing.com
website http://www.pc-publishing.com

First published 2009

© PC Publishing

ISBN 13: 978 1906005 108

British Library Cataloguing in Publication Data
A catalogue record for this book is available from the British Library

Printed and bound in Great Britain by Cromwell Press Group, Trowbridge, Wilts

Contents

Preface

This book is broadly divided into two sections: beginner and advanced. I decided to split the book because it made perfect sense to allow beginners to get to master the rudimentary techniques and theories involved in layering drum sounds and then to progress to more advanced techniques using dynamics, multi track layering and so on.

As with all my books and tutorials the premise is frequency based. In other words to understand sound and how to manipulate it you need to understand what the characteristics of sound are and how sound travels in a given space.

Although this book is not about mixing, and therefore how sound travels could be seen as a moot subject, it is essential to understand how sound is translated in a mix context and therefore very relevant when it comes to layering sounds, particularly in a drum beat scenario where we are actually mixing drum sounds to create the resultant beat.

The object of all my books is to afford the reader a three pronged attack on the way the information/content is presented: text, audio and visual examples have been shown to be the most effective method in translating information across, at least for me. I have always had a better chance of understanding and remembering a principle if it is presented to me this way.

The first part of this book concentrates on structuring projects, understanding frequencies, understanding how to manage frequencies with the tools available in audio editors, the dynamics of sound and its composites, and, finally, examples of layering techniques for different drum sounds and in unison (drum loops/beats).

The second part concentrates on dynamics and how to use them when layering drum sounds. There is also a section on stems and the tree structure and finally there's an assortment of project examples.

Each stage of this book has in depth audio and visual accompaniments and I hope they will go a long way in abating confusion when dealing with so many theories and techniques.

My primary audio editing software is Sound Forge 9. Please migrate the tools and procedures across to your own audio editor.

I would like to thank you for purchasing this book and hope the content will justify your expenditure.

Many thanks!
Eddie Bazil (Zukan)
www.samplecraze.com

Structure

As drum layering involves searching through vast libraries of drum sounds it makes sense to create some form of structure for easy access. At first it seems that there is no need to have any specific format or directory listings owing to the fact that the sample count is small and can therefore fit into a directory called 'drums' (this is how I began). But as time moves on and the library starts to expand it becomes evident that some form of structuring is required.

Creating folders for the drum elements is a good start. Kicks, hi hats and snares always have their own folders and that, at the very least, is a good way to further develop a hierarchy with sub divisions. By that I mean creating sub folders within folders. Kicks could then have sub folders called 'Acoustic Kicks', 'Synthetic Kicks', 'Sampled Kicks' and so on. The same can be applied to all the drum elements. However, when dealing with drum layering projects you need to take this methodology much further.

As we move further into this book you will realize that one of the most important techniques in shaping drum sounds is that of control over the dynamic envelope of the sound itself. This means that we can reshape the sound by clearly defined parameters. These parameters being: Attack, Decay, Sustain and Release and collectively known as ADSR (abbreviations). I will cover this subject in detail with theory and application but for now try to use these parameters in your structuring. Once you have created sub folders for each drum element it is extremely helpful to then create additional sub folders based on these parameter controls. So, let us take a kick drum as an example.

Main folder/directory: Drum Sounds
Sub Folder 1: Kicks
Sub Folder 2: Acoustic Kicks
Sub Folder 3: Attack
Sub Folder 4: Decay
Sub Folder 5: Sustain
Sub Folder 6: Release

Figure 1.1
The directory structure

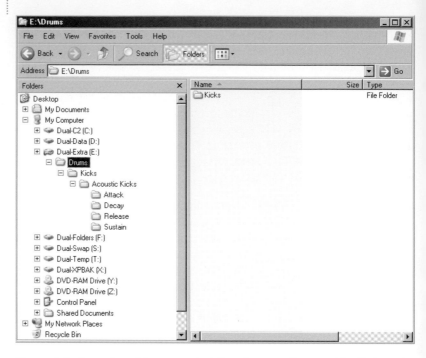

Figure 1.1 shows how I have created the directory Drums with all the relevant sub folders or sub directories.

You can add as many sub folders as you like both within another folder or stemming from the main directory (title folder).

The most successful way to create and define a structure is to work from a global directory and then to create sub folders that can be divided into further sub folders. Additionally, any folder can have its own 'tree' structure. A tree structure is simply a term used for this form of hierarchy. A tree has branches as do main folders and their sub folders. When you want to trace your ancestral history a family tree is usually what is depicted in terms of structure.

Running parallel folders with their own sub folders is the best way to organize sound libraries. In this instance the parallel folders for the main folder Drum would be Kicks, Snares and Hi Hats. This could be further defined by adding new folders and naming them appropriately. A good example would be a folder named Percussion. This folder could then contain sub folders for different types of percussive sounds. I tend to keep adding and adding and do not restrict myself. I have a parallel folder called 'Effected Drums'. This folder houses drum sounds that have been effected (reverb, chorus, distortion etc). This allows me to keep the dry (unaffected) sounds away from the wet (effected) sounds.

Part of the structuring process is correct labeling

I know how hard it is to name drum sounds because after a while it becomes hard to find names for sounds without being repetitive. But, at the very least, it helps to keep the terminology both simple and accurate. If a drum sound

Info

The more defined and accurate the labeling the easier it is to source a specific sound or parameter.

is from a specific kit or drum machine then naming it as such is very helpful, e.g. 909 Bass drum tone. Using this example you could then name further 909 drum sounds based on their duration, frequency, key location and so on. However, I am well aware that it is very easy to run out of names without ending up with hundreds of names starting with 909 Bass drum tone...

Certain drum sounds are easier to label than others and sometimes you simply need to get creative. Another way to label samples is to use the sample source: if the sample has been sampled from a record then the name of the record or artiste and the relevant track name etc could be used.

Structuring and sensible labeling are simply there to help you, and a little effort at the start of every project can save you acres of time and grief later.

Frequencies

Those who have read any of my other books will know that I hold one principle above all others: Understand frequencies.

To be able to understand sound, and how to process it in any context, a rudimentary understanding of frequencies is required. This does not mean that you need to hold a degree in physics, but it does require that you view sound in a slightly different way than the simple aural way.

The whole concept of layering is about layering frequencies. It does not matter what the 'sound' (in terms of labeling) is that is being layered. What matters is that frequencies are being layered and if you can bend your head around this simple statement then this book will be so much easier to digest.

Layering a bass sound with a kick sound relies solely on the frequency content of each sound and how they are presented and structured, and their interaction with each other. It makes no difference what the sound is in terms of labeling (bass, kick). What is important is what constitutes each sound's tonal character and content. We label sounds and categorise them for obvious reasons; to be able to distinguish one instrument from another, but I prefer to think in terms of frequencies because ultimately it is frequencies that are being managed. We will often say 'that bass needs some EQ' but when we come to apply the EQ it will be more akin to 'roll-off a few dBs at 300 Hz'. We are relating the process to a frequency/range and not the whole 'sound'.

The same applies across an entire mix. It is frequencies that are managed when producing/mixing a song. It is frequencies that are boosted and cut, separated and layered etc.

Although most drum sounds are short in duration, kicks and snares being good examples, people assume that they contain very little in terms of frequency content and therefore layering is simply about trial and error based solely on the perception of each sound. In other words; you may like the sound of one kick in isolation and another kick in isolation and the thinking is that both together will sound good. That is rarely the case. The thinking should encompass what each sound contains in terms of frequencies and how both sounds, once layered, will sound like. The premise here is not to layer sounds simply because they sound good on their own but HOW will they sound when layered. The objective is what we call the 'resultant' sound. This is the aim/goal/result we are trying to achieve and simply layering sounds that sound good on their own does not mean that this will be achieved. You will have far more success if you 'understand' what each sound can offer to the resultant sound once layered.

The above is as simple as possible: layering two like for like sounds (kick and kick); but imagine if you needed to layer more than two sounds, maybe three or four, and not necessarily like for like (kick, kick, tom and tabla). You can then imagine how complicated the whole task would become. The only sure fire way of dealing with this type of scenario is to think of all the sounds simply as frequencies. By understanding which component of a sound is required (ADSR) to successfully layer to other sounds then to think merely in terms of frequencies makes sense because realistically it is frequencies from different sounds that are being layered together, and by understanding which frequencies will complement each other and which frequencies will clash the task then becomes far easier.

The same applies to dynamic processing. When a sound needs treatment it is the frequencies that are being treated. For example: you would not say 'Boost the low end of that kick drum with EQ'. You would say 'Boost 50 Hz by 3dB'. This means that you are detailing the range that needs treatment by far more accurate terminology than a simple 'low end' statement. However, for simple referencing engineers will refer to allocated ranges in terms far more familiar. Low, mid and high are generally accepted terms used to define the tonality of a sound as a broad and pre determined range. A good example of this would be 'that mix needs a little more mid'. This simply means that the mix is lacking in mid range frequencies and needs to be boosted. In reality, we need to be more specific as to the range itself. Although accepted as a general form of communication for engineers the practical application is far more detailed and precise.

In terms of a sound the low end could be different to another sound. Let us take two kicks as an example. The low end of one kick might be a completely different frequency range to another kick but we still say 'low end'.

All this may seem a little pedantic and strict but when it comes to real life applications you will see how important specifics are and although the terminology is a form of generalization the actual referencing changes dramatically at the processing stage.

Sound

Sound is the displacement of air around the source and how we perceive that displacement.

Think of the best and most commonly used analogy: that of dropping a stone in a pond and watching the ripples form. The ripples always move away from where the stone meets the water (source). The 'air displacement' is the ripples created by the dropping stone. In this case we see the ripples. In the case of sound we hear the ripples (the displaced air).

How do we hear the displaced air?
Our eardrums pick up the displaced air and our brains then process the data as sound. What is important to understand is that there is a direct relationship between sound in the space it occupies and travels to/from and our interpretation of it.

Figure 2.1 illustrates how sound travels in a very simplistic fashion. The arcs/ripples are sound waves that move away from the source.

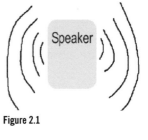

Frequency

This is simply calculated at how many cycles (waves) occur every second. These cycles are repeated so really we only need to look at how many cycles (waves) occur in one second. The result is measured as cycles/second and this unit of frequency is called a Hertz and the abbreviation is Hz. Figure 2.2 shows how a cycle is measured in terms of pressure and time.

Figure 2.1

Figure 2.2
The cycle nature of sound

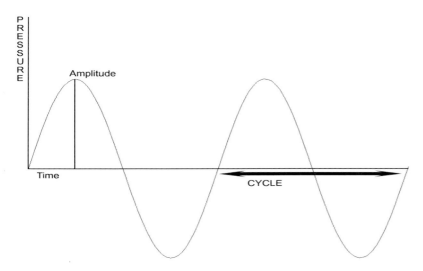

Using the waves/arcs analogy above think of each wave as a cycle and the amount of waves that are dispersed in one second are calculated as frequency. You cannot get simpler than that... how many cycles hit you in one second.

Heinrich Hertz was a clever chap who worked with wavelengths and frequency, so we have to thank the man and it seemed only right to name this little calculation after him. To give you an example of how easy this is consider the following example: If you had 50 cycles hit you in one second then that would be a 50 Hz wave.

So it also follows and makes complete sense that if you had 10,000 cycles per second then that would be 10,000 Hz, but, because we don't want to have to write so many zeros every time a thousand appears we use the letter k to denote a thousand. So, 10,000 Hz is now written as 10 kHz.

Range of hearing
And a range was formed; sure it varies but generally speaking, our hearing range lies anywhere between 20 Hz (low), to 20 kHz (high).

Now, let us think of that range and make life a lot easier by giving names you recognise to the frequency range.

So: bass, midrange and treble are easy to remember, and if you are old enough then that's about all that used to exist on hi-fi systems back in the days of armour and jousting.

Bass

10 Hz to 200 Hz. Also known as 'low-end'. Below approximately 10 Hz lies the 'feel' as sound is felt as opposed to heard.

Although it was, and still is to a certain degree, common practice to remove frequencies below 40 Hz when producing a mix this is more for low energy that can 'tire' the listener and make them feel a little ill to the stomach.

Listen to the following two audio files. One is at 10 Hz and the other is at 30 Hz. Although you can, or think you can, hear the 10 Hz file it is more felt than heard.

Figure 2.3
10 Hz sine wave

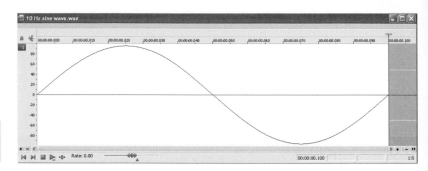

Sound file

10 Hz sine wave.wav

Figure 2.4
30 Hz sine wave

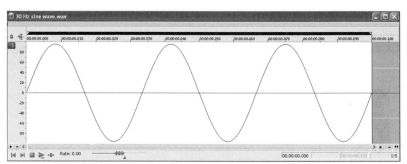

Sound file

30 Hz sine wave.wav

What is interesting here, and one to note, is that both waveforms are exactly the same length (0.10 seconds) and yet there are more cycles for the 30 Hz waveform than the 10 Hz waveform.

Looking at both images you might be thinking to yourself: 'how come there is only one cycle visible for the 10 Hz waveform and three cycles for the 30 Hz waveform?' Normally you would expect to see 10 cycles for the 10 Hz waveform (10 cycles/second) and 30 cycles for the 30 Hz waveform (30 cycles/second). But, because the lengths are 0.10 of a second (1/10 th) then we need to divide by ten. Basically, you are seeing a tenth of the amount of cycles that should be visible simply because I have created these two files at a length of a tenth of a second.

Had I supplied the full one second diagrams then it could be congested and you would not see the cycles clearly. But for the purists here below is the actual 1 second version of the 30 Hz file. Trust me, and if you are in the mood to count, there are thirty (30) cycles in that diagram.

Hopefully this makes the subject of frequency/cycles/time a little clearer.

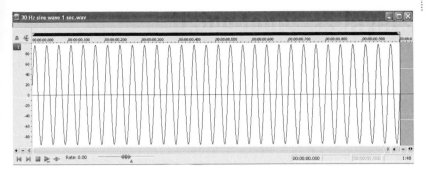

Figure 2.5
30 Hz sine at 1 second length

Sound file

30 Hz sine wave 1 sec.wav

Midrange or mid

A term you hear a lot of engineers use: 200 Hz to about 3 kHz. Also some-times known as 'high low' and 'low high'.

Treble

3 kHz to whatever is the highest value you can hear. Also known as 'top-end' and 'high-end'.

Above 14 kHz lies the 'air' regions, also known as 'space', 'presence' and 'sparkle'. This range deals with the very bright or high frequency ranges, and can also be felt as opposed to heard, much like the low-end.

The above are extremely general but will hopefully provide a ball park guide as to the three distinct hi-fi frequency ranges. Of course nowadays we have lots of very descriptive words defining specific ranges. However, the real importance of these basic ranges is to attune your thinking into understand-ing some of the terminology used when engineering a mix.

These ranges are often further defined with wonderful terms like 'boxy', 'nasal', 'presence', 'woolly' and so on. Understand the approximate frequency ranges and how they are described by engineers and you are halfway there in understanding how to then manipulate these ranges.

Possibly the most important piece of advice I can give in terms of fre-quency ranges is to always be proactive in listening to well produced and mastered material and then attuning both your ears and brain to under-standing the frequencies used and treated in a mix content.

Try to listen then gauge, listen then gauge.

If you feel the need then by all means use spectrum/frequency analysers to ascertain the frequency content of a sound or mix. Once you get to embed the varying frequency ranges of sounds in your brain (both in a mix context and in isolation) and then reference the values against your hearing, you will be in a strong position to recognise frequency ranges and how to treat them.

There is an area of thought and education that I would like to take a walk in. This is an area that deals with you on a personal level. It is the art of lis-tening. What you listen to and what you hear determine your tastes and per-ceptions about how a sound should be presented.

Like a studio with bad acoustics, how you hear a sound has a direct rela-tionship to how you think it should be portrayed. The same is true for the quality of the production of a given track that you listen to. If a track is pro-duced badly, your ears will accustom themselves to that track, and you will then try to mimic those qualities in your music. I always recommend that my

Tip

Try to listen then gauge, listen then gauge.

students listen to well produced music, even if it's not their taste or preferred genre. Attuning your ears and mindset to the right frequencies is crucial to a good mix.

In life we can only achieve a goal by having a reference point. That way we know if we have surpassed it or equalled it. Music is the same. If you listen to well produced music, your ears will attune themselves to the qualities inherent in the production, and your mindset will automatically take in reference points everywhere.

This will help you enormously in understanding what your sounds need, and in determining the types of frequencies that will be used in layering sessions.

Amplitude

Amplitude is the measurement of the displaced air (pressure), and in terms of audio this is perceived as loudness. Amplitude is actually the energy of sound or intensity/power. The level or intensity of an audio signal (i.e. the loudness) is measured in decibels (dB) using the dB scale. 'Deci' being a tenth and 'Bel' being the unit.

You may be wondering why we measure in tenths and not in single units. Our ears can hear a vast number of audio levels and it would be a mathematical nightmare to try to use the 'actual' numerical representations of audio levels - so we use tenths to make it easy to understand and calculate.

The true definition of dB is far more complicated and relative to ratio, logarithm of the ratio between two power levels etc, but all I want you to understand is that we measure audio level in dB.

The simplest way of explaining dB in terms of both hearing and measuring is to use the following:

Total silence is expressed as 0dB on the decibel scale. So if you had a sound that was ten times more powerful then it would be expressed as 10dB. That should be easy to understand. Where it gets a little confusing is that if you had a sound that was 100 times more powerful than total silence, it would be measured as 20dB. A sound 1000 times more powerful would be 30dB and so on. We basically work on a logarithmic scale when dealing with dB.

However, I will keep it very simple and stick with dB as simply being a way to measure loudness/level. If I state that at 30Hz I boosted by 3dB, then that means that the gain knob was moved up by 3dB at that frequency.

I wanted to give a slightly detailed explanation of dB and not just to state it as a measurement, but to go any deeper than the above would be both confusing at this juncture and not relevant to the subject matter.

I have deliberately stayed away from defining the components of sound as that subject is covered in detail in my book *Sound Equalization Tips and Tricks* available from PC Publishing.

You may be thinking that the above is a little irrelevant when it comes to layering drum sounds but without the understanding of frequencies and how we measure them it would be very difficult to understand the second part of this book which deals with dynamic processing tools, effects and advanced applications.

ADSR: attack, decay, sustain and release

Every sound has a shape and that shape is defined by frequency, amplitude and time. Two of the three components can be displayed in the form of a physical diagrammatical representation and they are volume against time. This representation is called the 'amplitude envelope'.

I make this distinction because there are different envelopes for different functions. An example would be the 'filter envelope' used in sound synthesis to shape the filter response or 'shape' over time.

Within this envelope we break sound down into simple components that are used to shape the sound. In terms of sound design, or simple reshaping, we break down the control of sound into certain pre defined parameter controls: Attack, Decay, Sustain and Release (see margin pic) .

The sound waveform starts at 0, rises to its peak point, drops to the sustain (body) and then tails off on release. Imagine if each of these parameters were moved either up or down to control volume or left to right to alter time, you would then be simply reshaping the sound.

The beauty of this is that any area of the sound can be reshaped irrespective of the others. The best way to explain this is with a simple example.

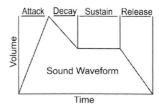

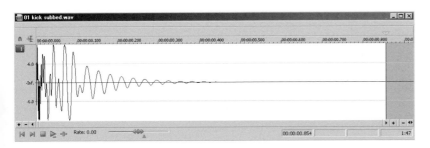

Figure 3.1
A kick drum unaffected

Sound file

01 kick subbed.wav

Figure 3.2 shows the Envelope tool accessed through the main menu in Sound Forge, sub menu Effects. This is my default ADSR template.

The jagged dark content is the waveform representation. The lighter blue lines are the ADSR parameters and each one has a 'node' which is used to reshape the shape. The reshaping is achieved by moving the nodes to their desired positions. At the moment the ADSR shape is very similar to the shape denoted top right. Sound Forge allows further nodes to be created and used. However, I have kept it simple with the standard 4 node template.

Additionally, please make sure to select the correct option in 'Show Wave'

Figure 3.2
The Envelope tool accessed through the main menu in Sound Forge, sub menu Effects

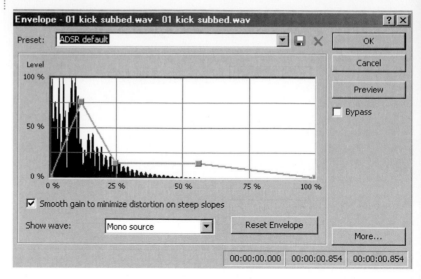

(currently selected as a Mono source due to the waveform being in mono). This will change when we deal with a stereo waveform. Figure 3.2 shows that I have ticked the 'smooth gain to minimize distortion on steep slopes' option. I did this to smooth out the attack response. Had I left it intact the attack would have sounded harsher. In the snare example (Figure 3.5) I deliberately unticked this option to allow for the attack to be kept intact.

I will now reshape the sound by moving the nodes (Figure 3.3).

Figure 3.3
Sound reshaped as nodes are moved

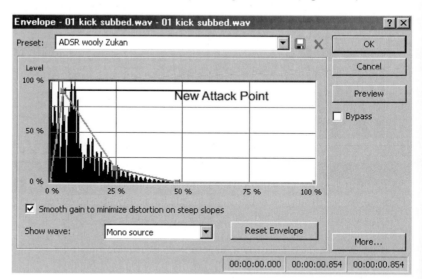

If you look carefully at the reshaped ADSR above you will notice that I have moved the attack point across to the right in the timeline. I have done this deliberately to avoid the hard attack of the sub kick and to soften the attack and move it across to the next peak point. By removing most of the attack and having a strong decay dropping down to the sustain I have not only shortened the sound but made it much softer.

Figure 3.4 shows the new shape of 01 kick subbed. Not only has the waveform (sound) been reshaped but the sound has dramatically changed.

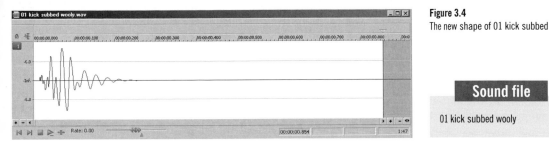

Figure 3.4
The new shape of 01 kick subbed

Sound file

01 kick subbed wooly

Sometimes, all you need to do to expand your drum library is to simply reshape existing sounds and save them as new sounds.

I will give one more example of this technique on a snare sound. Figure 3.5 shows the unaffected shape of a snare sound.

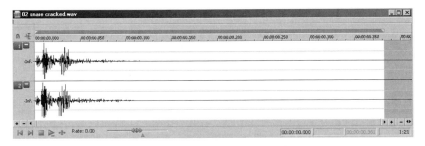

Figure 3.5
Unaffected snare sound

Sound file

02 snare cracked.wav

Figure 3.6 shows the reshaped template I have created for the snare sound. I have moved the attack to a new location almost abating the whole of the original attack. But the real power of this reshaping comes in the very steep decay that almost kills the whole of the attack sound and keeps the sustain very short with a negligible release. The waveform is not completely reshaped and sounds very different.

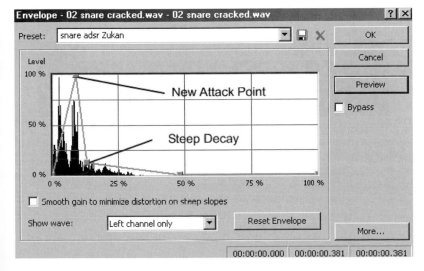

Figure 3.6
Reshaped template

Figure 3.7
Options available in Show Wave

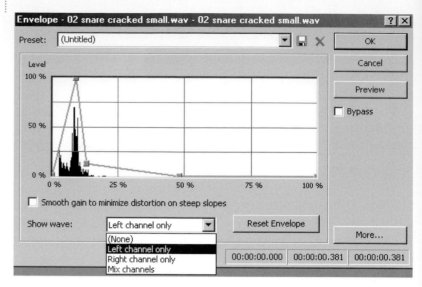

As mentioned earlier it is important to select the correct option in 'Show Wave'. In this instance you can select the Left, Right and Mix channels to process as the waveform is in stereo. Figure 3.7 shows the options available in Show Wave.

Figure 3.8
The new shape

Sound file

02 snare cracked small.wav

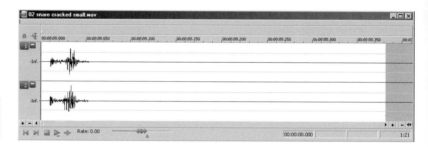

Figure 3.8 shows the new shape. What really stands out here is not just the new shorter sound that has been created, but the movement of the attack. If you look closely at the image above you will see how far the attack has been moved compared to the image in Figure 3.5.

Feel free to experiment with as many different types of waveforms as possible as this will help you to instinctively make the right option selections which in turn will optimize the sonic result of any waveform.

The ADSR tool is an invaluable one and the primary tool used to create individual ADSR components from existing waveforms that later go to form the basis of the layering examples given in this book.

Creating ADSR components

In Chapter 1 we touched on the subject of structure and how to create folders and sub folders for the ADSR components. A folder for attacks, one for decays and so on ensures that you have a readymade library that you can tap into when layering different parts of a waveform onto another. There are two ways to achieve this:

- Cut, paste and tail off (fade out)
- ADSR tool

Let us go through both methods briefly and ascertain the pros and cons of each. I am going to start with a kick example and select components from the waveform and create new waveforms of each component.

Cut, paste and tail off

In real life examples it is useful to understand where one component ends and another starts. For example: the decay of the attack of a waveform might 'intrude' into the sustain (body) of the same waveform. The same can be said for the sustain 'intruding' into the release of a waveform. The decision as to which ends and which begins is really down to personal choice.

The usual way to ascertain which component ends and which one starts is to search for peak and drop points within the waveform but as this is merely a guide it only serves a useful purpose when dealing with sounds that have clearly defined components. But, ultimately you might like the attack of a sound and also some of the decay and sustain and this will then become a single component when edited. So the idea of sticking to a strict format is not always the right choice and this is why the more you experiment the more you will gain in terms of understanding, instinctively, what the right decision is to make.

Figure 4.1 shows a newly selected waveform. I am now going to select the

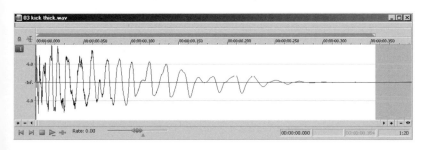

Figure 4.1

Sound file

03 thick kick.wav

Figure 4.2
The attack component highlighted

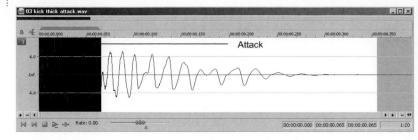

Sound file

03 thick kick attack.wav

attack, body and release of this kick and show you where the selection for each component is. You will note that I left out the decay component. I did this because the kick drum I have selected has got a very small decay from the attack and therefore both components blur into oblivion. Figure 4.2 shows the attack component being highlighted.

Attack

By using the copy/paste function and copying the highlighted section into a new file I am able to separate the attack component from the original waveform and create a new waveform that is then labelled and saved as 03 thick kick attack into a sub folder. Figure 4.3 shows the new attack waveform.

Figure 4.3
The new attack waveform

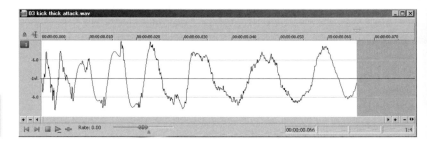

Sound file

03 thick kick attack.wav

We have now created a new waveform of the attack but it does not end there. Please try to edit your waveforms so as to remove any anomalies like abrupt releases. We call this process 'top and tail'. Originally, this term referred to the old school sound design technique for normalizing a sample and then fading out the release. Simply highlight the area that needs fading out and select the 'fade out' function in the Process menu (Figure 4.4).

Figure 4.4
Select 'fade out' in the Process menu

Sound file

03 thick kick fade out.wav

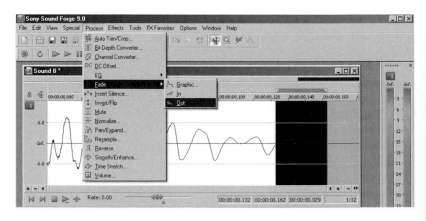

If you now listen to the newly faded out attack waveform you will notice that the sample end (release) is much smoother and has no noise or abrupt ending.

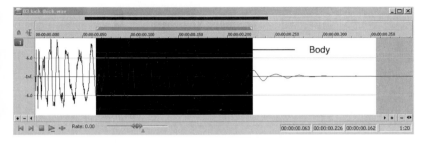

Figure 4.5
The sustain component

Sustain

Let us now create a new waveform for the body (sustain) of the 03 thick kick waveform. Figure 4.5 shows the sustain component I have highlighted. If you look carefully at the waveform you will notice that I have deliberately selected the sustain (body) start point at the 0 (zero) axis. I have done this so that the body does not have an abrupt start or display clipping if selected halfway through a peak point. This makes for a much smoother start point for the sustain and the body will sound as if it is a waveform in its own right.

I suggest you experiment with different start points for the sustain and release components so that you can see and hear how different start points affect the start of a sound. Much as we use fade outs for the sample ends we need to be careful when deciding where a sample starts at the extraction stage (copy/paste).

Figure 4.6 shows the new waveform created using the copy/paste command and then fading out the end exactly as before.

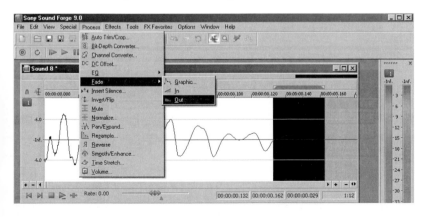

Figure 4.6
The new waveform

Sound file

03 kick thick body fade out.wav

Release

Figure 4.7 displays the release component (end). This is the component that needs to be accurate in terms of start points.

The release of any waveform should be a smooth transition from start to end. Selecting a poor start point for the release will make layering a nightmare.

Figure 4.7
The release component

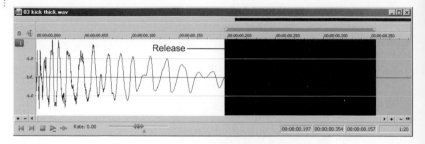

The best option is to select a start point at the 0 axis as this means that the release waveform now starts at 0 and then climbs to its own new attack peak. It doesn't matter how short a sample is and whether it is an edit (extraction) from another sample, the same components will exist. The release has its own ADSR exactly as its source sample.

If a 0 crossing is hard to locate then you can use the 'fade in' option for the start of the release waveform as this will smooth out any abrupt attacks. I will cover both. Figure 4.8 shows the new release waveform extracted from a 0 axis crossing.

Figure 4.8
The new release waveform

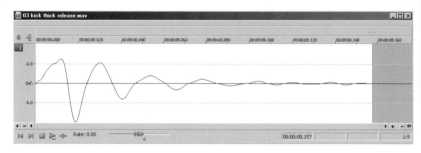

Sound file

03 kick thick release.wav

An important point to raise at this juncture is that of 'gain' or volume. ADSR components can either display strong or low gains. Depending on the type of sound, the attack by its very nature will always have the strongest gain value in the waveform. The sustain will invariably have a lower gain value and the release will generally display the lowest gain value.

The release waveform of the kick waveform is pretty low in gain so I boosted it by a simple normalization process to bring it up to a healthy level so that when it comes to layering I am not using a low gain waveform that then has to be boosted within the new layered waveform. Try, simply as habit, to check the gain values of all the components you extract. This makes gain management much easier when it comes to the layering process.

Figure 4.9

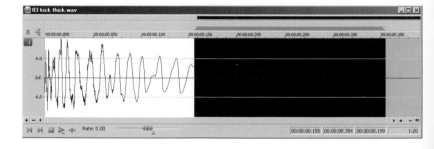

And now let us look at the release that starts partially into the waveform peak, i.e. a non 0 crossing point. Figure 4.9 shows a non 0 crossing waveform. I will now create a new waveform from this source waveform and show you where the release start begins (Figure 4.10).

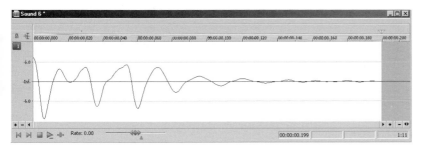

Figure 4.10

Sound file

03 kick thick release non zero crossing.wav

Figure 4.10 clearly shows the non 0 crossing start. The short click (anomaly) sound is evident at the start of the release waveform and this is not desirable as it will be heard when layered. It is best to resolve this problem at source and not later as it will be a lot harder to both isolate and then process amongst other layering waveforms.

You can either use the 'fade in' function, much as we did with the fade out by highlighting the area that needs fading in and then simply selecting the function, or use a graphical fade in, which is what I prefer as it gives you far more control on the shape of the fade in.

You can select the graphical fade function (both in and out) from the main menu Process/Fade/Graphic and Figure 4.11 shows what it looks like, and if you look closely you will notice that it is another ADSR tool but used for creating fades.

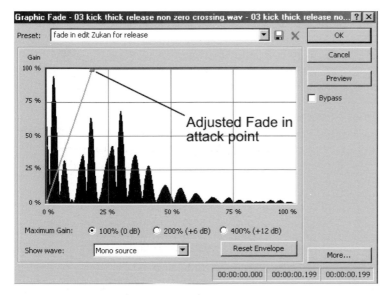

Figure 4.11
The graphical fade tool

I have highlighted the node that I have moved beyond the click sound (anomaly) to create a much smoother fade in.

Figure 4.12
The new waveform after rendering the graphical fade in

Sound file

03 kick thick release non zero crossing graph fade in.wav

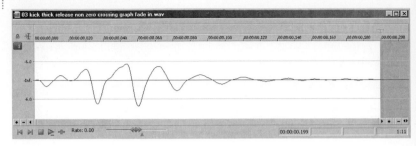

Figure 4.12 shows the new waveform after rendering the graphical fade in. The result is a much smoother attack to the release.

I would now like to show you how to achieve the above but by using the ADSR tool.

Using the ADSR tool

The process is a little different in terms of procedure as the component is not being extracted but the original waveform gets overridden by the component. In other words we are working on the same waveform and reshaping it.

With this in mind I always create a copy of the original waveform and work on the copy so the original stays intact as a source file so I can keep using it to create the other components. Additionally, the fade in and out functions are already inherent in the ADSR tool itself so we can perform all fades in unison with the reshaping.

Let us use the same kick sample and try to replicate, as closely as possible, the attack extraction using only the ADSR tool. Figure 4.13 shows the ADSR tool and the shape I have created using the nodes available.

Figure 4.13
The ADSR tool

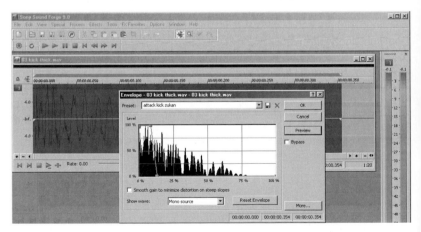

Figure 4.14 shows the resultant waveform. If you look at Figure 4.14 you will notice that there is a lot of 'dead space' (air as it's commonly known) after the waveform itself, unlike the extracted attack waveform in Figure 4.3. The reason for the huge difference is that the waveform in Figure 4.3 is the whole waveform of the extracted area whereas the waveform in Figure 4.14 is a reshape of the entire source waveform and will include all data.

In this instance it is important to note that any dead space needs to be truncated (cut/removed) otherwise this redundant area will affect the layering process.

Figure 4.15 shows how to truncate dead space. Simply highlight the dead space after the sample end and right click to open up the edit menu and select cut. Figure 4.16 shows the result of the truncation.

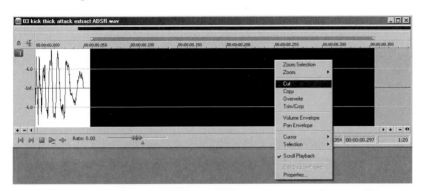

Figure 4.15
Truncating dead space

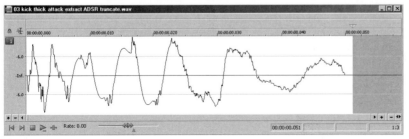

Figure 4.16
The result

I prefer to use the ADSR tool to create the individual components as it allows for reshaping any section of a waveform and boosting certain areas if needed. It also allows for much easier 'real time' auditioning whilst editing than trying to cut and paste and then retrying.

Let me briefly show you how to create a completely new shape that will sound very different to the original source waveform.

Figure 4.17
The ADSR tool with a new shape

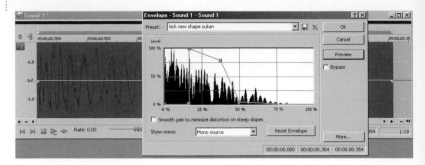

Figure 4.17
The ADSR tool with a new shape

Figure 4.17 shows the ADSR tool with a new shape I have created using the nodes.

When using nodes you are not limited to just moving them across the x-axis (left/right) but also, as we did earlier, vertically on the y-axis (up/down). This means that we can either boost by moving the node up or attenuating (lowering the gain value) by moving the node down.

I have chosen a section that incorporates the decay of the attack into a section of the sustain and by moving the nodes upwards I have boosted the attack section of this new area and applied a gradual decline (attenuation) in the gain towards the release.

Figure 4.18 shows the result of the reshaping. The dead space before the sample starts is clearly exhibited in the ADSR tool shape in Figure 4.17 and the little dip after the sustain and before the release is also evident as is the release itself.

Figure 4.18
The result of the reshaping

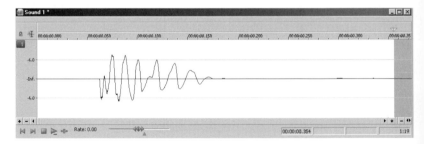

Because we have applied the new shape to the entire source waveform you will have dead space wherever a node is moved to 0, so please take care to truncate and edit out any dead spaces as this will then help greatly when it comes to the layering process.

Figure 4.19 shows the resultant layer after truncating the dead space before the attack of the new waveform and normalizing the entire waveform to bring the gain value up closer to the ceiling. This new waveform sounds very different to the original source waveform.

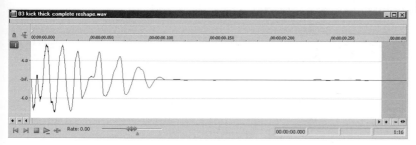

Figure 4.19
The resultant layer

Sound file

03 kick thick complete reshape
trunc norm.wav

This and the previous chapter are two of the most important chapters in this book as understanding, and successfully achieving, extractions and reshapes of the ADSR components is critical when it comes to correct layering tasks. If, for example, an attack is poorly edited and presented then it will have a negative overall effect on all the layers or components used.

Please feel free to experiment as much as possible because the more you experiment the more your brain and ears will attune themselves to how certain frequencies 'sound' and decision making will then become instinctive as opposed to trial and error.

As with all tools there is always something out there that might suit the way you work better than the suggested tools in this book. However, the theories and methodologies presented in this book are important; please make sure to understand and apply them before venturing into deeper waters.

ADSR extraction layering examples

We have covered, in detail, the two different methods of extracting ADSR components. However, it does not end there as there is still one more method used when layering drum sounds and it does not involve extracting components. We will cover this in the next chapter.

What I would like to do now is to run through some examples of using both methods covered to layer sounds and create a new resultant sound.

Cut and paste

I am going to use two kick sounds and use the attack from one waveform and the body and tail (sustain and release) from the other to create a third sound; the resultant layer.

The trick, as mentioned before, when using the cut and paste technique is to make sure that the start and end of each waveform that is being edited is aligned at the 0 axis otherwise there will be anomalies. However, what is even more important is the shape of the start and end of each waveform because when adding one waveform (sustain) to another waveform (attack) you need to make sure the shape of the resultant waveform is both smooth and in the right direction.

Let me explain this visually and aurally. Figure 5.1 shows the two opened waveforms in Sound Forge with the highlighted areas that are to be cut and pasted to create the resultant layer.

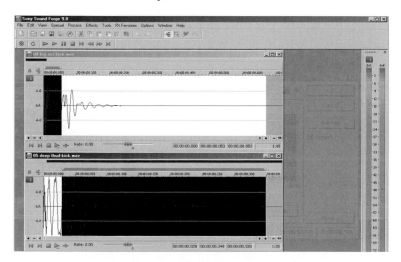

Figure 5.1

Sound files

04 big ass kick.wav
05 deep thud kick.wav

25

The highlighted areas are the areas I am going to cut and paste together. I am going to use the attack from the 'big ass kick' waveform and the body from the 'deep thud kick' waveform. I am now going to cut each section and open them in separate windows (Figure 5.2). This shows the new waveforms created by using 'highlight (the area), copy and then paste'.

Figure 5.2

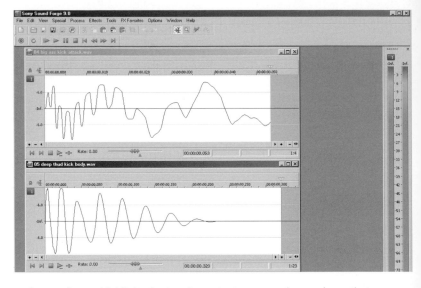

Sound files

04 big ass kick attack.wav
05 deep thud kick body.wav

I am going to highlight the two important areas and zoom in so that you can see how the waveforms progress from where I have cut them (Figure 5.3).

Figure 5.3

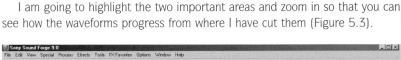
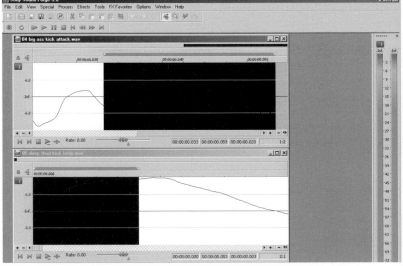

In the top layer (waveform) the release of the attack has been highlighted and in the bottom layer I have highlighted the attack of the sustain (body) waveform. As you can see both of these waveforms cross the x axis (obviously) at 0 points. The trick is to create the resultant layer with both waveforms smoothly following each other with no breaks or 'staggers'.

To create the smooth and unbroken waveform we need to make sure that each waveform joins the other in the same direction, and the easiest way to do this is to select a 0 axis crossing and to make sure to use the correct direction.

In Figure 5.4 I have drawn vertical lines to show the 0 axis location that I want to cut and paste at, and you can see that both waveforms are ascending below and above the x axis.

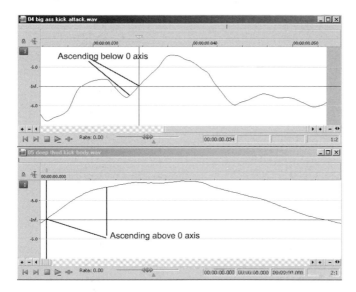

Figure 5.4

If we now cut the area after the 0 crossing for the attack waveform (top) and before the 0 axis for the sustain (below) and then paste the two together we should get a smooth resultant layer. Figure 5.5 shows zoom of join between the two waveforms into the new waveform.

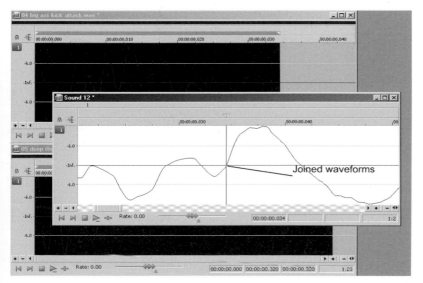

Figure 5.5
The join between the two waveforms

Figure 5.6
The resultant layer

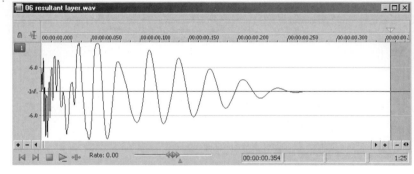

Sound file

06 resultant layer.wav

Figure 5.6 shows the resultant layer final shape. The join cannot even be seen as it is so smooth and the audio file represents a nice and flowing resultant layer with no abrupt ends and starts or any anomalies.

I am now going go through the same procedure but without editing the waveforms crossings and joining the attack and sustain where the initial cuts took place.

Not only does the waveform look disjointed but it also exhibits an obvious anomaly when auditioned. So long as you make sure that the joins are smooth and flowing in the same direction you should end up with a good result.

Figure 5.7
The poor join in the resultant layer

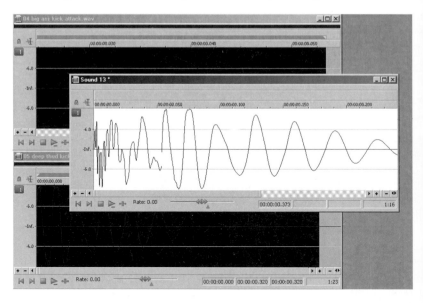

Sound file

07 cut and paste poor join.wav

The pencil tool
While we are on the subject of cutting and pasting poor joins we might as well touch on a great little editing tool that is available on almost all audio editors. It is the 'pencil' tool. The pencil tool allows you to draw in waveforms wherever you see fit.

Using the example above I am going to 'redraw' the join into a fluid and smooth shape as opposed to the 'jagged' and 'staggered' shape currently shown. You need to zoom in to the area that is the join and redraw the waveform at the join so as to allow a smoother join.

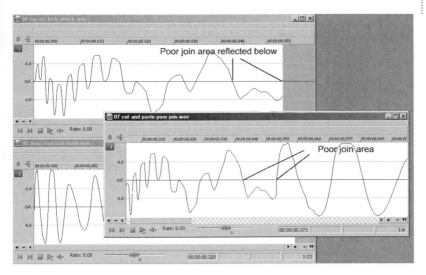

Figure 5.8
The poor join area

By lining up the waveforms, one above the other, it makes it much easier to locate the join area. You can see where the joins are in both the wave-forms.

Figure 5.9 shows where I have redrawn the poor join to be a smoother and more fluid join. Once I render this file you will see the new shape (Figure 5.10).

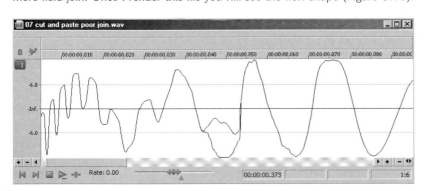

Figure 5.9
The poor join area redrawn

Sound file

08 cut and paste redrawn wv.wav

If you listen to the redrawn waveform the anomaly (poor join) has disap-peared and the resultant waveform sounds smooth again.

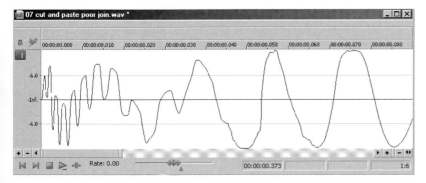

Figure 5.10
The new shape

ADSR envelope reshapes

Let us now concentrate using the ADSR method outlined in the last chapter. The thinking is the same as the cut and paste technique but the application is a little different as we have detailed earlier. We will use the same two kick waveforms. Figure 5.11 shows the ADSR tool being used to create the attack component of the 'big ass kick' waveform.

Figure 5.11
The ADSR tool being used to create the attack component of the 'big ass kick'

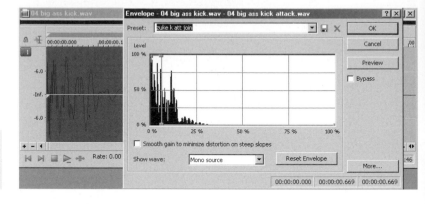

Sound file

09 big ass kick adsr join attack.wav

Figure 5.12 shows the ADSR tool being used to create the sustain component of 'deep thud kick' waveform.

Whereas before, with the cut and paste method we cut and pasted the two waveforms one after the other, with the ADSR technique we simply mix the two waveforms together to form the resultant layer.

Figure 5.12
Creating the sustain component of 'deep thud kick' waveform

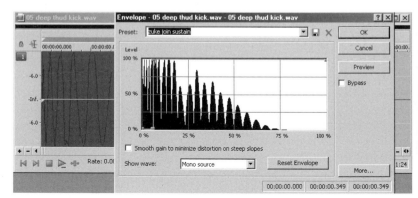

Sound file

10 deep thud kick adsr sustain.wav

Figure 5.13 shows the two layers being mixed, and Figure 5.14 shows the resultant layer which when compared to Figure 5.6 looks and sounds almost identical.

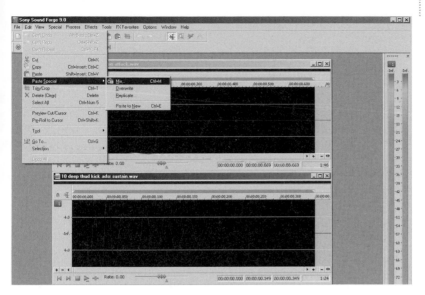

Figure 5.13
Mixing the two layers

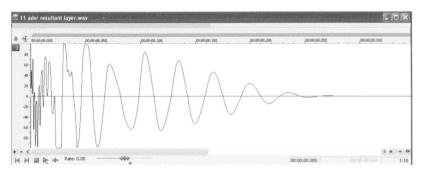

Figure 5.14
The resultant layer

Sound file

11 adsr resultant layer.wav

The techniques covered in this chapter are more important than any other type of layering techniques simply because of the accuracy and flexibility afforded. Of course, there is the standard whole waveform layering method that many use only because they have never been aware of these two simple techniques. And it is the entire waveform layering technique that I want to explore with you in the next chapter.

As with all the examples, theories and techniques in this book practice is the only way to instinctively develop an understanding and feel for which techniques to use in any given situation.

Layering entire and complete waveforms

The most common method of layering drum sounds is that of layering entire waveforms. In the days of memory restricted hardware samplers, sound designers would treat each layer as a voice and edit each voice as we have done in the previous chapter, in other words, using ADSR reshapes and cut and paste techniques to shape each layer to complement each other.

With the lack of editing skills that so many possess today and the sheer volume of ready made sample libraries available to all, the art of layering has ended up as a long lost skill. Most people now search for a drum sound they like, find another one and so on and then try to layer them all as one single resultant layer. They then try to shape the resultant layer with EQ and compression.

Before we jump into some examples I feel it is important to point out the two main shortcomings associated with this particular technique. The first is frequency related and includes clashing, summing and masking. The second deals with the timeline and size of the waveform.

Layering frequencies

When layering drum sounds it is often with the intent of using certain frequencies from one sound that are appealing and layering those frequencies with the frequencies of another sound that are also appealing. However, when these frequencies are not separated and are simply layered one on top the other then a number of anomalies will appear.

Clashing

This occurs when certain frequencies from source layers do not marry well or complement each other to form a harmonic resultant layer. They end up sounding 'wrong'. This is called clashing, i.e. frequencies that sound out of place when used together. This can reveal itself in the form of noise, frequency mush, phase etc.

You often hear this term used when certain sounds in a mix simply do not sit together well.

Summing

When two shared (the same) frequencies (from different layers) of the same gain value are layered you invariably get a boost at that particular frequency. This form of summing can be good if intended or it can unbalance a layer and make certain frequencies stand out that were not intended to be prominent.

A good way around this problem is to leave ample headroom in each waveform file so that when two or more files are summed they do not exceed the ceiling and clip. In terms of an audio signal, headroom is the difference between the maximum signal level and the maximum limit of its environment/device.

In the digital domain we know that the ceiling is 0 dBFS, and anything beyond this incurs digital clipping. When using extracted ADSR components the headroom is not affected as much as entire waveform layering simply because each component is already at a pre determined level and placed at different timeline locations in the resultant waveform. However, as ADSR components often overlap it is still important to take into account the headroom available and not to eat into it too much.

Additionally, ample headroom is required when we come to applying dynamics to a waveform. Dynamics, by their very nature, control gains and invariably are used to boost levels (compression, EQ etc). Any form of a gain boost will eat into the headroom.

Masking

When two shared frequencies are layered and one has a higher gain value than the other then it can 'hide' or 'mask' the lower gain value frequency.

How many times have you used a sound that on its own sounds excellent, but gets swallowed up when placed alongside another sound? This happens because the two sounds have very similar frequencies and one is at a higher gain; hence one 'masks', or hides, the other sound. This results in the masked sound sounding dull, or just simply unheard. A common example, in a mix context, is when a high range piano sound might be masked by a high range string sound. The same problem applies when layering drum sounds. The sustain (body) of one waveform might dominate and mask the body of another waveform when layered together.

Sensible use of filters and dynamics with a good understanding of gain management usually resolves this problem. We will come to this later in this book as dynamics and effects have a pronounced effect on frequencies and gain values.

Timeline and size of waveforms

Every waveform is measured as amplitude by time. In other words, when looking at any of the examples used in this book you will see that a waveform is represented as time across the x axis and amplitude across the y axis (Figure 6.1).

The 'length' of the waveform is displayed horizontally from left to right and the amplitude is measured vertically. Amplitude we have already covered in

Figure 6.1
The x and y axis displaying time and amplitude

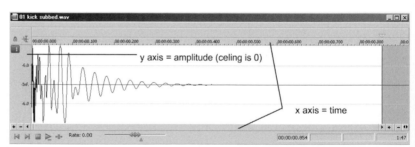

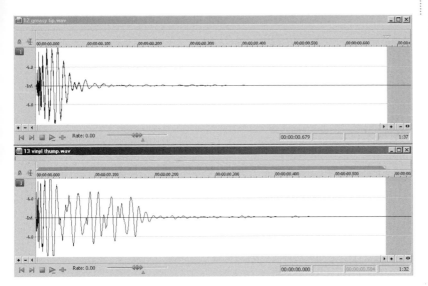

Figure 6.2
Two waveforms with different wavelengths

Sound files

12 greasy tip.wav
13 vinyl thump.wav

terms of headroom but even more important is the wavelength.

When layering two waveforms the time factor becomes crucial as varying lengths will exhibit a mismatched resultant layer. The best way to explain this problem is with an example.

If you look across the x axis you will notice that both waveforms have different wavelengths. They both exhibit different ADSR components as well. By layering both waveforms, complete and as they are, to create a new resultant layer, the issue of both time and amplitude comes into consideration.

As both waveforms peak at near to 0 it is easy to deduce that once summed they will exceed the ceiling and clip. As before, create a third envelope so that the two waveforms can be mixed and summed into it to create the resultant layer. By using the menu options Edit / Paste Special / Mix the waveforms can be mixed to a new resultant layer. Take a careful look at the meter readout in Figure 6.3 which clearly shows exceeded gain values of the two summed waveforms.

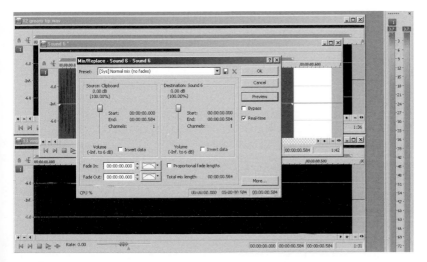

Figure 6.3
The Mix tool and the meter readout

Figure 6.4
The two source layers and the resultant
layer

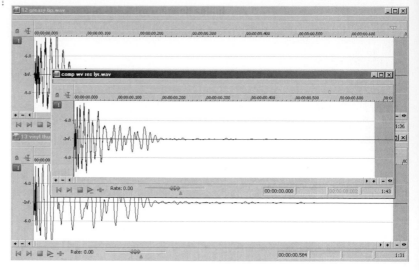

Sound file

16 comp wv res lyr.wav

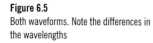

The Mix tool allows for the gain value of each waveform to be adjusted so that when summed they will be below the ceiling.

To render these two waveforms without exceeding the peak you simply move the source and clipboard gain values until the desired level is attained. I have made sure to keep both waveform gain values identical no matter how much I reduce (attenuate) them.

Masking

The following example will concentrate on masking and for this we will use two clap waveforms that are very different in terms of time and frequency content (Figure 6.5). However, one of the waveforms shares a lot of the frequencies with the other and when mixed will be almost inaudible.

Figure 6.5
Both waveforms. Note the differences in
the wavelengths

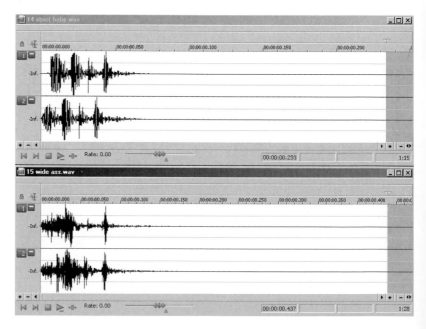

Sound files

14 strict baby.wav
15 wide ass.wav

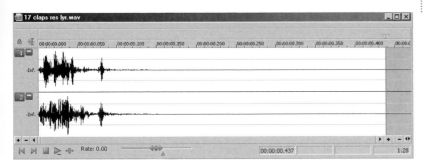

Figure 6.6
Masking

Sound file

17 claps res lyr.wav

Using the same Mix tool and adjusting the gain values equally the resultant layer will clearly display what masking is. The resultant layer (Figure 6.6) looks completely different to both waveforms but sounds very much like 15 wide ass.wav because 15 wide ass.wav has masked 14 strict baby.wav.

Layering entire waveforms can be a very useful process so long as one of the waveforms exhibits different sonic qualities. In the event that the same waveform is layered with a copy of itself, as some people like to do, then it is helpful to understand what actually takes place.

When the same sound is layered onto itself the gain values are summed and it is a misconception to assume that frequencies are added to or subtracted from. One of two things happens: the gain values are summed if both waveforms are used with equal peak values or one waveform is masked if the gain value is lower at the layering stage.

The real power, when layering the same waveform onto itself, is when the sonic characteristics of one of the waveforms is altered either via an ADSR reshape, or via a dynamic process which we will cover later in detail. However, for now, I would like to show you a quick example of this using a simple filter to change the frequency content of one of the layers and then to use the Mix tool to create a resultant layer (Figure 6.7).

Figure 6.7
The same waveform copied with the Blue Filter being applied to one of the layers

Figure 6.8
The original unaltered layer and the copy layer that has been filtered

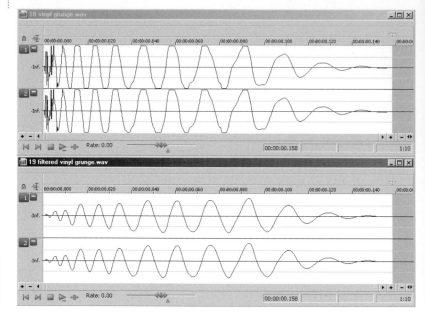

Sound files

18 vinyl grunge.wav
19 filtered vinyl grunge.wav

And by creating a third envelope and using the Mix tool it becomes easy to vary the gain values and create a new sonic waveform as the resultant layer.

Figure 6.9
The two waveforms (one copied) and the Mix tool with the varying gain values

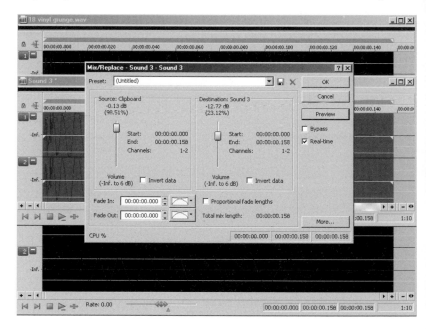

Figure 6.10 shows the resultant layer.

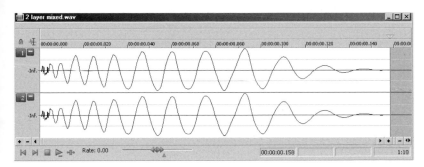

Figure 6.10
The resultant layer

Sound file

2 layer mixed.wav

Later on in this book, when we explore dynamics and effects, I will go into far more detail and provide more working examples.

Using tones as layers

A common technique in layering drum sounds is to use tones or 'sounds' as layers. This is not a new concept and has been around for a long time. In fact, this process has been used in sound design when creating instrument presets by using multi layers of certain waveforms. Using tones when layering drum sounds is a very potent way of creating a new sonic flavour, whether it is a new sound entirely or enriching certain frequencies. However, the process is not simply about using any tone as a layer but using a tone that has been sensibly created with frequencies in mind. Waveforms and frequencies go hand in hand.

A midi to frequency chart can be invaluable here as it can show you what frequencies note values have. Most people know that A4 displays a frequency of 440 Hz. Knowing this actually gets you quite far in understanding what frequencies to use in layering. The chart below shows most of the frequency values for the corresponding note values I have supplied so that you will have a reference to use.

This may all seem a bit pointless to you but it is very important when it comes to working examples. You have often heard people use the term 'tuning the drums' or 'tuning the kick to the key of the song'. This is done so that the drum sounds do not clash with the song. It is also crucial to tune a drum kit so that each drum sound is not out of tune with the kit. The same thinking applies when layering drum sounds particularly when using tones.

A common sound design trick is to layer a kick drum with a sine wave tone so as to add 'low end'. In fact, this is how most sub kicks are designed. The TR 808 sub kick is tone based so understanding frequencies and how to create tones is your saviour here.

N	Midi Note	Frequency	N	Midi Note	Frequency
A0	21	27.500	F4	65	349.228
A#0	22	29.135	F#4	66	369.994
B0	23	30.868	G4	67	391.995
C1	24	32.703	G#4	68	415.305
C#1	25	34.648	A4	69	440.000
D1	26	36.708	A#4	70	466.164
Eb1	27	38.891	B4	71	493.883
E1	28	41.203	C5	72	523.251
F1	29	43.654	C#5	73	554.365
F#1	30	46.249	D5	74	587.330
G1	31	48.999	D#5	75	622.253
G#1	32	51.913	E5	76	659.255
A1	33	55.000	F5	77	698.456
A#1	34	58.270	F#5	78	739.989
B1	35	61.735	G5	79	783.991
C2	36	65.406	G#5	80	830.609
C#2	37	69.296	A5	81	880.000
D2	38	73.416	A#5	82	932.328
D#2	39	77.782	B5	83	987.767
E2	40	82.406	C6	84	1046.502
F2	41	87.307	C#6	85	1108.730
F#2	42	92.499	D6	86	1174.659
G2	43	97.999	D#6	87	1244.507
G#2	44	103.826	E6	88	1318.510
A2	45	110.000	F6	89	1396.913
A#2	46	116.541	F#6	90	1479.978
B2	47	123.471	G6	91	1567.982
C3	48	130.813	G#6	92	1661.219
C#3	49	138.591	A6	93	1760.000
D3	50	146.832	A#6	94	1864.655
D#3	51	155.563	B6	95	1975.533
E3	52	164.812	C7	96	2093.004
F3	53	174.614	C#7	97	2217.461
F#3	54	184.998	D7	98	2349.318
G3	55	195.997	D#7	99	2489.016
G#3	56	207.652	E7	100	2637.020
A3	57	220.000	F7	101	2793.826
A#3	58	233.082	F#7	102	2959.955
B3	59	246.942	G7	103	3135.963
C4	60	261.623	G#7	104	3322.437
C#4	61	277.183	A7	105	3520.000
D4	62	293.664	A#7	106	3729.310
D#4	63	311.127	B7	107	3951.066
E4	64	329.628	C8	108	4186.009

Create a tone using Sound Forge

As the first example in this chapter I am going to show you how to create a tone using Sound Forge. This tone will then be used as a layer to add low end to an existing kick waveform.

In Sound Forge you need to select Tools / Synthesis / Simple. Figure 7.1 shows the Sound Forge Synthesis tool and Figure 7.2 shows the Synthesis tool and its menu options. The menu options are very simple.

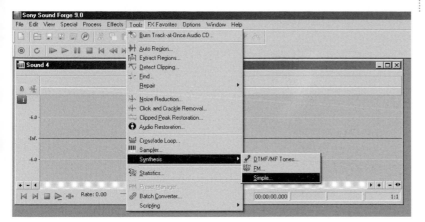

Figure 7.1
The Sound Forge Synthesis tool.

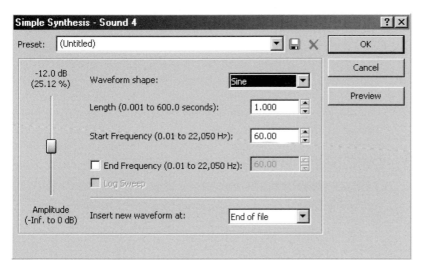

Figure 7.2
Synthesis tool menu options

- You can select the Waveform Shape you want from a drop down menu that includes Sine, Absolute Sine, Square, Saw, Triangle, Filtered Noise, White Noise, Pink Noise and Brown Noise.
- Length selects the wavelength.
- Start and End Frequencies are only important when creating sweeps. For our examples we will only need Start Frequency as we want a consistent and static waveform.
- On the left is the Amplitude fader which sets the gain value of the waveform.

I am now going to create a simple sine wave and by using the frequency chart I can set the frequency I desire. As I am going to create a sub kick I will select 32.7 Hz as the frequency so as to default to a C1 note value with C being the most common key used in music.

Figure 7.3 shows the settings I have created for the waveform. I have set the wavelength at 0.5 seconds, the frequency at 32.7 Hz and the amplitude at -0.7 dB.

Figure 7.3
The settings I have created for the waveform.

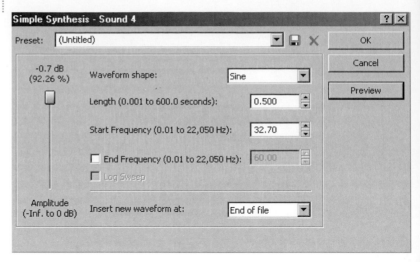

I have kept the wavelength short because I am aware of the drum layer I am going to use and any more than half a second would have been excessive. You need to decide beforehand what would constitute an adequate wavelength for the project in mind. You might find that you are layering to create a long fading sub kick and a longer wavelength would be obviously more suitable in this instance.

These settings will give me a healthy sine wave tone at a note value of C1 with a strong gain value. Figure 7.4 shows the new waveform.

Figure 7.4
The new waveform

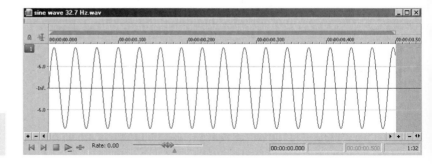

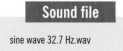

Sound file

sine wave 32.7 Hz.wav

At this juncture you have two choices: do you apply an ADSR reshape to the sine wave or do you simply use it as is and layer with the kick waveform? The answer to this depends on what you are trying to achieve and what you 'hear' in your head as the resultant sound. I will cover both possibilities.

For now I am going to use the sine wave as it is and layer it with 20 tight.wav. Figure 7.5 shows the two different wavelengths.

By placing one above the other and assessing the wavelength it is far easier to make the decision about whether to apply ADSR to the sine wave now or to layer as is. I am going to go ahead and use the Mix tool and create a resultant layer using the sine wave as is.

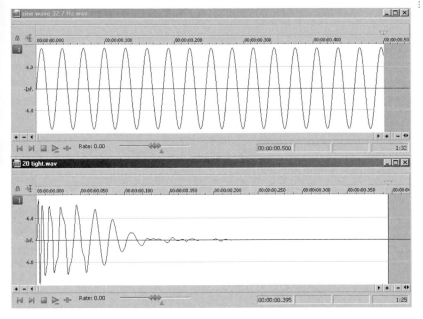

Figure 7.5
The two different wavelengths

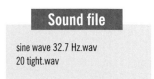

Sound file

sine wave 32.7 Hz.wav
20 tight.wav

Figure 7.6 shows the gain values I have selected to best layer the two waveforms.

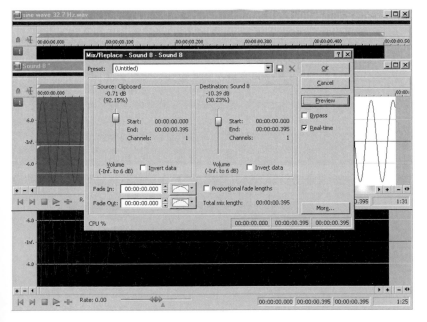

Figure 7.6
Select the gain values

Figure 7.7
The resultant layer

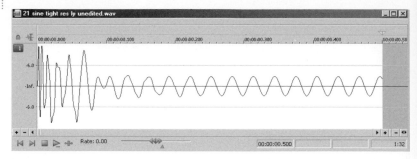

21 sine tight res ly unedited.wav

Figure 7.7 shows the resultant layer. At this point you can reshape the resultant layer by using any of the techniques covered earlier, but whichever process you use please remember to use fade outs where needed as this waveform has a poor end and needs a fade out.

I am going to use the ADSR tool and shape the resultant layer. Figure 7.8 shows the ADSR shape I have created and Figure 7.9 shows the resultant reshaped layer.

Figure 7.8
The ADSR shape I have created

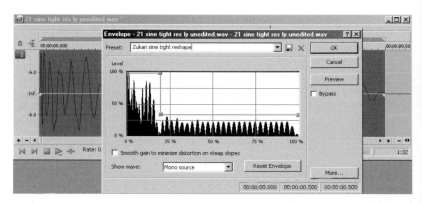

Figure 7.9
The resultant reshaped layer

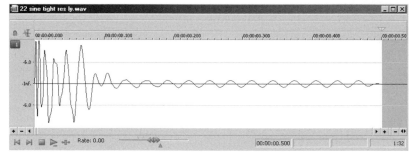

22 sine tight res ly.wav

You can clearly hear the tone beneath the kick sound and the two together make for a really rounded sub kick tone.

Kick sample

In the next example I am going to use a kick sample that already sounds full and usable but it is in mono and, although kick drums tend to be in mono, due to the fact that they need to occupy a central position in the mix, it can be extremely useful to understand how to create a stereo width feel without compromising the integrity of the sample.

There are ways of creating stereo width for kick drums and the natural method is to record it in stereo or to use a dynamic that outputs the resultant file in stereo. But to understand any of these processes it is important to realise that simply converting a mono file into stereo by duplicating one channel onto another does not add any sonic qualities, and all that happens is that two mono channels now exist, in fact this is called dual mono. A mono sample is a single channel of information and a stereo sample is two channels of information.

To best express this, the following example duplicates one channel of information onto another and a dual mono file is created. The tool being used in Sound Forge is the Process / Channel Converter (Figure 7.10). We will now process this mono channel into a dual mono file even though the process claims it to be stereo (Figure 7.11).

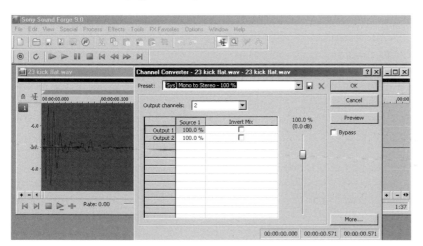

Figure 7.10
The Channel Converter tool in Sound Forge.

Sound file

23 kick flat.wav

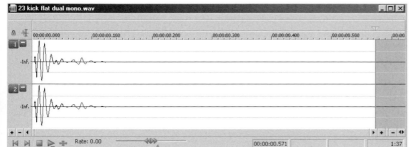

Figure 7.11
Processed 'stereo' file (dual mono)

Sound file

23 kick flat dual mono.wav

As you can clearly hear from the sound file, there is absolutely no difference between the two sounds although the file information has been doubled. If I were to now vary one channel's information, even by a tiny amount, then you would hear both channels as true stereo.

Creating stereo image and width

A trick I am going to use is an old one and it works in creating a stereo image and width. This is not a hidden secret but a method a lot of engineers and sound designers have used. It simply entails changing the timing information of one channel by the tiniest amount. The ear then perceives the difference

Figure 7.12
The difference between the two channels

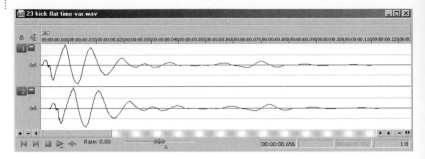

23 kick flat time var.wav

and sums the sound as stereo. I am going to do this crudely so you can clear-ly hear the difference between the two channels (Figure 7.12).

I have copied one of the channels onto a stereo file and then copied the same channel onto the next channel but added a tiny timing variance which I have zoomed to show the difference.

Adding space and depth with noise

However, for our layering example I am going to use a 'noise' waveform, which we will create using the Synthesis tool, and layer this with the kick to add space and depth. In this example we need to think about the noise fre-quency that we are going to use. The kick does not possess very low fre-quency data so it really comes down to trial and error by using your ears.

But first a little bit about 'noise'. I think this is important and relevant as the Synthesis tool in Sound Forge has options for using different forms of noise.

In essence, noise is a randomly changing, chaotic signal, containing an end-less number of sine waves of all possible frequencies with different amplitudes. However randomness will always have specific statistical properties. These will give the noise its specific character or timbre. If the sine waves' amplitude is uni-form, which means every frequency has the same volume, the noise sounds very bright. This type of noise is called white noise. If the amplitude of the sine waves decreases with a curve of about - 6 dB per octave when their frequencies rise, the noise sounds much warmer. This is called pink noise. If it decreases with a curve of about -12 dB per octave we call it brown noise.

White noise is used in the synthesizing of hi-hats, crashes, cymbals etc, and is even used to test certain generators. Pink noise is great for synthesiz-ing ocean waves and the warmer type of ethereal pads. Brown noise is use-ful for synthesizing thunderous sounds and deep and bursting claps. Of course, they can all be used in varying ways for attaining different textures and results, but the idea is simply for you to get an idea of what they 'sound' like. And this can only help when it comes to layering.

For our layering example I am going to use 'Filtered Noise' for the wave-form because the amplitude is affected by the frequency. This allows me to select a frequency for the waveform. If you were to try any of the other noise options within the Synthesis drop down menu you would see that none of the frequency options appears.

Let us now create a noise waveform using the Synthesis - Simple tool (Figure 7.13). If you look carefully you will notice that I have input a fre-quency value of 65.40 and if you were to check this against the Midi and Frequency chart at the start of this chapter you would see that a frequency

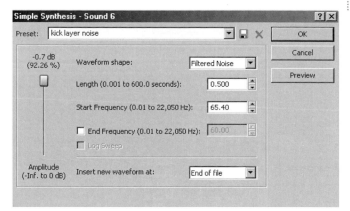

Figure 7.13
The Synthesis Tool with the Filtered Noise settings

Sound file

filtered noise wf.wav

of 65.40 Hz equates to a note value C2. I chose this only because I knew that it would be a good starting point for this example. You can, of course, select whatever frequency you want but try to keep it at the relevant frequency and not some random figure. This makes further processing far easier to assess and execute. Figure 7.14 shows the created waveform.

By using the Paste Special/Mix a new layered waveform is created (Figure 7.15).

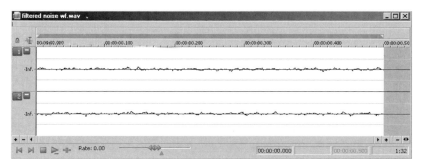

Figure 7.14
The created waveform

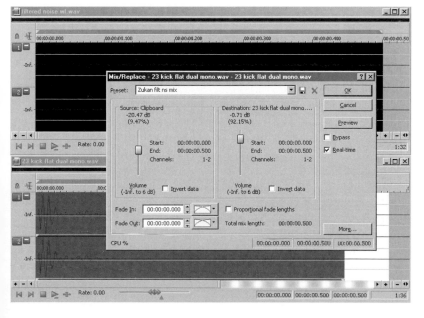

Figure 7.15
The Mix values selected

Figure 7.16
The resultant waveform without any editing

Sound file

23 kick flat ns layer.wav

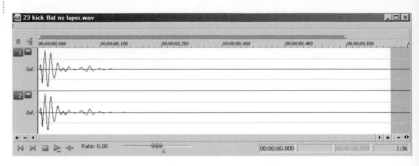

Figure 7.16 shows the resultant waveform without any editing, and Figure 7.17 shows the envelope tool reshape.

Figure 7.17
The envelope tool reshape

Sound file

23 kick flat ns layer.wav

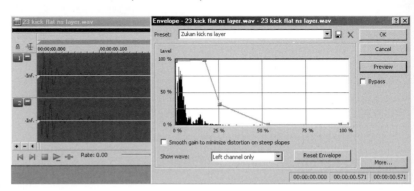

All that is left to do now is to shape the resultant file using the ADSR envelope tool and then truncating the dead space afterwards (Figure 7.18).

Figure 7.18
The resultant truncated file

Sound file

23 kick flat ns layer truncated.wav

The resultant file now sounds more spacious offering depth and width without compromising the original file's sonic qualities.

Layering a snare sound

I would like to do one more example but using a snare sound that is pretty rich in mid to high frequencies. The reason for this is that I want to show you how important gain structuring is when layering waveforms like noise.

I have created a dual mono file of the snare and have created a stereo file for the noise waveform (Figure 7.19). I have input a frequency of 2093 Hz (2.093 kHz) which equates to a note value C7. I have also brought the amplitude right down so that it is in the background. Selecting a high frequency

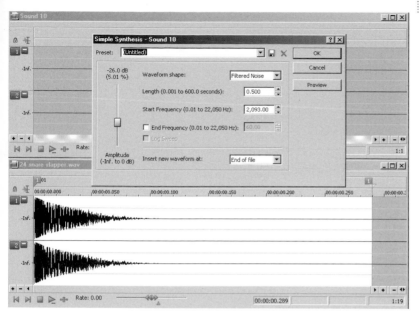

Figure 7.19
Both files and the settings for the noise creation

Sound file

24 snare slapper.wav

value is important when dealing with a snare that possesses high frequency content and we are doing this so as to add ambience to the sound as opposed to a lower frequency selection which would not have been subtle but would have been prominent.

Figure 7.20 shows the Paste Special / Mix tool and Figure 7.21 shows the envelope tool being used to shape the snare's tail to give the perception of 'space'. The snare now sounds more spacious and 'alive'.

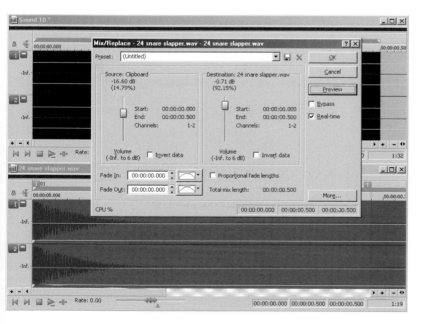

Figure 7.20
The Paste Special / Mix tool

Figure 7.21
The envelope tool being used to shape the snare's tail to give the perception of 'space'

Sound file

24 snare slapper ambiance.wav

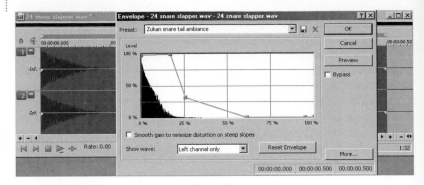

Using noise to create space without having to re-record sounds with microphones to gain ambience, or to use reverb etc, is a great technique that has been used by mix engineers for a long time.

This technique does not stop with kick and snare sounds. It is highly effective in adding depth and space to toms, hi hats and just about any drum and percussive sounds.

Adding a brown noise layer

For the next example I am going to show you how we can take a simple short tom sound and add brown noise as a layer to give the sound both depth and space. However, where this example differs from previous ones is that we need to further edit the brown noise to complement the sonic qualities of the tom. There is no point in trying to marry two layers together if they sound distinct on their own as what we are trying to achieve is fluidity and consistency in how the sound is perceived.

Dynamics, as we will discover later, are great tools to use to shape and colour an existing sound and in this example we will use a filter to 'darken' the brown noise sample so that it is consistent with the tom's sonic qualities. Figure 7.22 shows the dry tom waveform.

Figure 7.22
The dry tom waveform

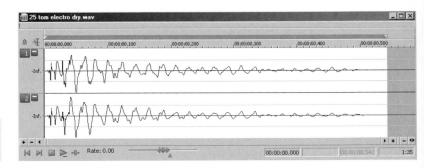

Sound file

25 tom electro dry.wav

The tom sample is pretty short and quite thick, but let us add more depth and space and reshape it to make it consistent and natural sounding. To do this we need to use the Synthesis tool again and this time we will use brown

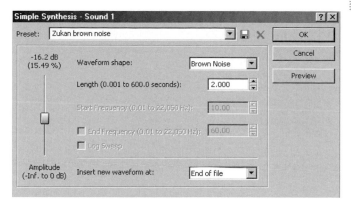

Figure 7.23
The Synthesis tool being used to create the brown noise waveform

Sound file

synthesis brown noise.wav

noise for our layer. However, once we have created the brown noise file we need to alter its texture to comply with the tom's sonic qualities, and for this we will use a filter.

Be careful when selecting a gain value (amplitude) for the brown noise because if it is too loud then it will sound distinct and obtrusive, too low and it will disappear when layering. I like to select a mid value or just below a mid value, as my goal is to use the noise layer to create ambience and space. Additionally, when using the Paste Special / Mix tool you can adjust the levels for the source and destination. Figure 7.23 shows the Synthesis tool being used to create the brown noise waveform.

Figure 7.24
The parameters I have created for this example

Sound file

blue filter brown noise.wav

For the purposes of layering the brown noise with the tom we need to treat the brown noise file to make it sound darker and with less high frequency content. For this we will use the Blue Filter (Figure 7.24).

If you study the Blue Filter settings you will note that the most important parameters that have been adjusted are the Filter Mix, Frequency and output Gain. The Lfo section is disabled as we are only concerned with frequency and gain management for now.

The next step is to mix the two waveforms and adjust the gains, if necessary, to attain the desired effect and level for the resultant file (Figure 7.25).

Figure 7.25
The adjusted gain structuring of the source file (brown noise waveform)

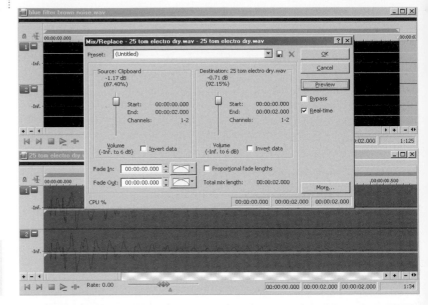

Sound file

25 tom electro brown noise mix unedited.wav

Figure 7.26
The settings for the envelope tool

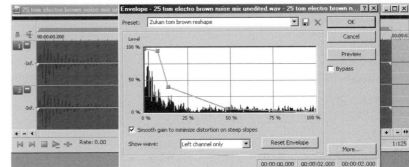

Sound file

25 tom electro brown noise mix.wav

We now need to apply the envelope tool and shape this resultant file. The tom now sounds far deeper, more spacious and has a lovely tail off (fade out). You can, of course, shape the resultant file any way you want.

Creating new textures

So far, we have used noise to create depth, space and width but we have not touched on creating a completely new texture by shaping noise and then layering it with another sound.

Figure 7.27

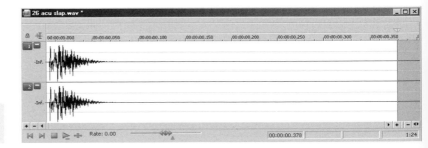

Sound file

26 acu slap.wav

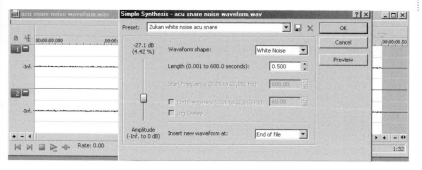

Figure 7.28
The setting used to create the white noise waveform

Sound file

acu snare noise waveform.wav

Figure 7.27 shows a thin and lifeless snare that has been channel converted to dual mono. By using the Synthesis tool we can create a white noise waveform so as to complement the frequency content of the snare (Figure 7.28).

Before we use the Paste Special / Mix tool to mix the two waveforms it is useful to shape the noise waveform into a shape that is similar to the snare waveform and complements it.

This is different to the normal method of mixing two waveforms and then reshaping the two together as we have done previously. The reason for this is that we are trying to actually create two individual percussive sounds and then to layer both their sonic qualities into one resultant file to create a new texture, as opposed to 'adding a quality' to one layer. Figure 7.29 shows the envelope tool reshape for the white noise waveform.

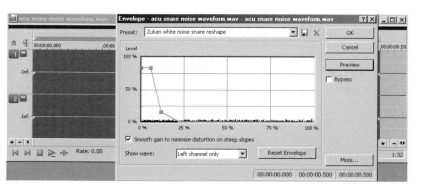

Figure 7.29
The envelope tool reshape for the white noise waveform.

Sound file

acu snare noise waveform reshape.wav

This waveform now sounds like a distorted, or electro, snare and will work well with the layering task. The mix tool is shown in Figure 7.30. The resultant file sounds completely different to the original acu snare file and is thicker, deeper and wider.

You can create any texture you want simply by adjusting the sonic qualities of either waveform, reshaping them, mixing them and so on.

Figure 7.30
The mix tool

Sound file

26 acu snare white noise mix.wav

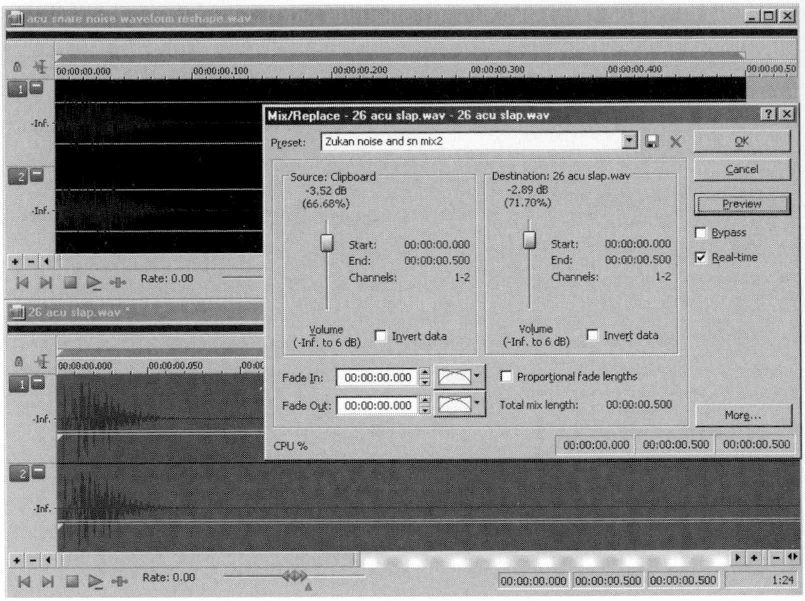

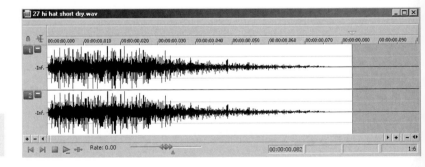

Layering a hi hat sound

The next example I am going to explore in this chapter is one that entails a hi hat metallic sound that will be layered with a triangle waveform. I am going to create two versions of the same goal. The first one entails a short lifeless hi hat that needs to be livened and the second example will be a triangle sound that is very short that needs extending. This will allow us to explore different frequency layers for each example.

Triangle waveforms are good for creating bell type and metallic sounds and are perfect for hi hats and percussive sounds that have metallic sonic qualities. I am going to take a very dry and short hi hat sound and layer it with a high frequency triangle waveform so as to add life and a little more body and tail to the resultant waveform.

Figure 7.31
The short dry hi hat waveform

Sound file

27 hi hat short dry .wav

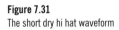

The hi hat sound is very dry and short and sounds a little lifeless. The next step is to use the Synthesis tool and create a triangle waveform with a frequency that matches the hi hat.

I have selected a midway amplitude, a short duration (length) and a frequency of 8372 Hz (8.372 kHz) which equates to a C9 note value. Although the C9 value is not on the chart I provided at the start of this chapter it is

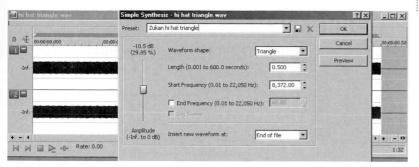

Figure 7.32
The Synthesis tool parameter selections

Sound file

hi hat triangle.wav

still very simple to work out what the next octave from C8 would be in terms of frequency as all that is needed is to double the C8 frequency to attain the next octave (C9). Doubling 4186 Hz gives me a frequency of 8372 Hz.

The next step is to mix the two waveforms and then reshape the resultant waveform using the envelope tool, much as we have been doing in previous examples.

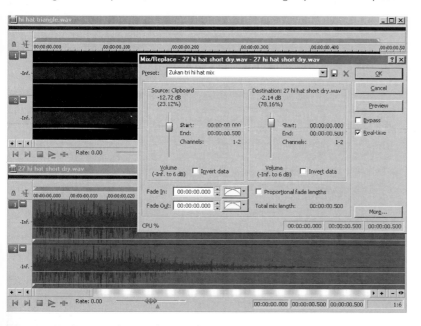

Figure 7.33
The mix tool and the settings I have input to get a good balance between the two waveforms

Sound file

27 hi hat triangle mix.wav

We now need to use the envelope tool and reshape the resultant waveform.

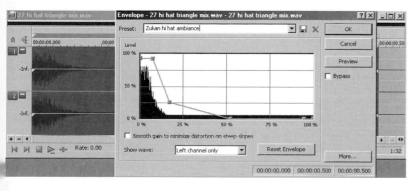

Figure 7.34
The shape of the envelope

Sound file

27 hi hat triangle reshaped result.wav

The final waveform sounds far more alive and spacious simply by using a basic triangle layer.

Layering a short triangle sound

Let us now explore another example but this time we will use a lively but short triangle sound and layer it to extend its body and tail so as to give it a little more life and ambience.

Figure 7.35
The short triangle

28 short triangle.wav

Using the synthesis tool we will create a short triangle waveform at a frequency of 2.093 kHz which equates to C7 note value (Figure 7.36).

Figure 7.36
The values selected to create the triangle waveform

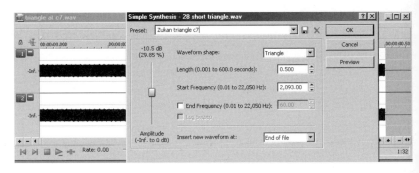

Sound file

triangle at c7.wav

The next step is to mix the two waveforms and then to reshape the resultant layer. Figure 7.37 shows the mix values.

Because a midway value was selected for the waveform at the synthesis level, mixing the two waveforms becomes a far simpler and more balanced process. In this instance the original triangle sound was already rich and vibrant so making the amplitude/gain adjustment for the synthetic triangle waveform becomes even more critical. You can, of course, experiment as much as you like as all these processes can be reversed. Figure 7.38 shows the envelope shape created for the two layers.

The resultant waveform has a slightly fuller body and longer tail and still sounds rich and lively.

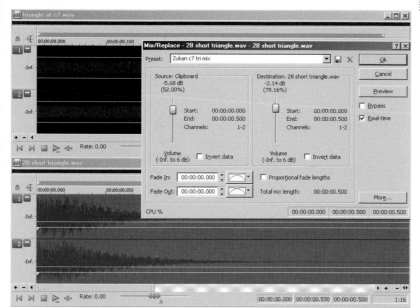

Figure 7.37
The mix values

Sound file

28 short triangle and c7 triangle
mix.wav

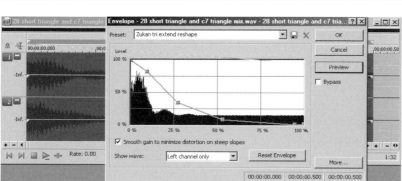

Figure 7.38
The envelope shape created for the two
layers

Sound file

28 short triangle and c7 triangle
reshaped.wav

Feel free to try as many variations as possible. It is only through extensive trial and error that your ears and brain will form reference points and future layering projects will become easier and easier to conquer.

- Using synthetic waveforms to create new sonic textures has been a tried and trusted technique used by most sound designers.
- Do not ignore the value of using simple synthetic waveforms for layering projects.
- Explore different waveforms at different frequencies and lengths and try to be creative irrespective of how extreme the results may seem.
- Only through continual experimentation will you develop a strong sense of 'what sounds right' and you will probably find new ways of manipulating synthetic waveforms for layering projects.

Dynamics: compression

No drum layering book would be complete if the two most important dynamics were not covered: compression and equalization.

In this chapter we will cover compression not only in terms of what it is and how to use it but with working examples to help to demystify the whole process for you.

Compression – why use it?

The simplest way to describe the function of a compressor is as follows: a compressor makes the quiet bits louder and the loud bits quieter. It acts as an automatic volume control.

Before the advent of workable compressors engineers used to adopt a method of volume control called Gain Riding. This was simply a term used for the manual process of moving a fader on a mixer up and down to control the varying levels of the audio passing through it. But this was never too accurate, as you had to anticipate when the audio would rise or drop in gain and make the necessary adjustments in real time. However, with the introduction of the compressor the gain riding process could now be automated and with far greater control and detail.

Today, compressors have become creative tools as well as dynamic controllers. In fact, it is fair to say that compressors, certainly in the mainstream pop and dance markets, have become almost mandatory requirements for the mix and production processes. Sadly, a great many producers and mastering engineers have abused this invaluable tool and more and more commercial releases suffer from what we call the 'square wave' syndrome whereby the audio is so compressed that the peaks and troughs of the audio waveform collapse closer together and create a square shape. However, this is a completely separate subject in itself and one that will be covered in another book.

The most common use for a compressor, in terms of drum layering, is that of sonic reshaping. In effect, the compressor is used to reshape the ADSR of a waveform to exhibit a completely new sonic texture. Additionally, the gain structure invariably changes and it is usually here that many stumble. We will explore this area, along with the sonic reshaping, as we proceed with examples of drum compression. However, before we delve into detailed examples, it is important to understand how a compressor works and what each parameter control offers.

Threshold

This is the input level above which compression occurs. Above this level, the output increases at a lesser rate than the corresponding input stage.

Set the threshold high to compress only the loudest part of the signal, set it low to compress more of the signal.

Ratio

This is the ratio of the change in input level to the change in output level. For example, a 2:1 ratio means that for every 2 dB change in input level, the output changes 1 dB. A 'soft-knee' characteristic is a low compression ratio for low-level signals and a high ratio for high-level signals. With infinite setting, the output stays the same no matter how much you increase the input.

Attack

This is how fast the compressor reduces the gain when a signal is input. Basically, the time it takes to activate itself. Longer attack times mean that more of the signal goes through, before it starts to get compressed.

Release

This is how fast the compressor returns to neutral, or how fast the gain returns to normal. Short release times give the famous 'pumping' or 'breathing' sound, and are good for following rapid gain changes. Long release times sound more natural and don't interfere with the sound's harmonics.

Gain reduction

This is the number of dB that the gain is reduced by the compressor, and varies with the input level. This is displayed on the meter.

Side chain

Mainly available on hardware compressors but now more popular amongst their software counterparts, the side chain function is used for inserting an EQ or filter, or any device, into the signal path, independently of the main input signal, so that the compressor responds only to frequencies boosted by the input device/signal, in this case the EQ.

The EQ does not affect the actual input signal, only the controls of the unit, the controls then adjust the main input signal. They can also be used creatively and make for some great effects.

Output control or gain makeup

Because we are squashing peaks in the signal, we are actually reducing the overall peak level, increasing the output level compensates for the volume drop. Turn this level up until the peak levels of the compressed signal match the bypassed signal peaks.

Peak/RMS

RMS stands for root mean square and is a mathematical term for a method of averaging the level of a complex waveform. If your compressor has a Peak/RMS switch, this will determine how the compressor evaluates the incoming sound level and your choice for selection is dependent on the type of material you will be compressing. The beauty of using RMS is that we, as humans tend to use this method for listening. Our ears average out incoming audio, so RMS works in the same way.

But, as stated, the method chosen is dependent on the audio being processed. For short signals, such as drum sounds, Peak will work much better. In Peak mode, the compressor takes action based on the peak level of the input signal, no matter how long or short the sound is. In this instance, using a fast attack time and the Peak setting will afford far better sonic control over the audio than RMS.

I tend to find that RMS works really well on longer, undulating sounds, like vocals, and Peak works well on short sounds, like percussion.

Knee

Knee refers to the way the compressor reacts when the input level reaches the threshold. A hard-knee compressor brings in all the gain reduction as soon as the signal crosses the threshold. A soft knee on the other hand brings in the compression more progressively by gradually increasing the compression ratio as the signal level approaches the threshold. Again, the choice is down to the material being processed.

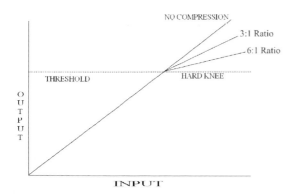

Figure 8.1
Hard knee compression

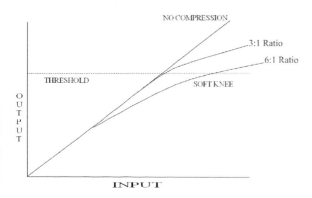

Figure 8.2
Soft knee compression

Now let us take a brief look at the different types of compressors.

Stereo/dual channel compressor

If a compressor is to be used on a stereo track, it is important that a stereo compressor or dual channel compressor be used. Dual channel compressors feature a stereo link switch that effectively sums the two channel levels together and then uses this combined signal to control both channels. In this way, the same gain reduction is applied to both channels at all times. If the two sides worked independently, then the compressor would sound as if it were shifting from side to side, as audio will vary in loudness from channel to channel.

When linked for stereo operation, both channels of the compressor react to a mix of the sound passing through the two channels so both always react together, regardless of the level balance between the two channels.

Multiband compressor

These divide the incoming audio signal into multiple bands, with each band being compressed independently from the other. The beauty of this is that with full band compressors, which we have been discussing till now, the whole signal is treated, so when a peak is detected, the whole signal is compressed and so other frequencies are also subject to compression.

Multiband compression compresses only the frequency bands chosen, so a more fluid and less abrupt result is gained. Instead of having one peak trigger the compressor into compressing the entire signal, the multiband allows for individual bands to be compressed. On some compressors, you even have the option of selecting bands that will not undergo any treatment.

In essence, a multi-band compressor comprises a set of filters that splits the audio signal into two or more frequency bands. After passing through the filters, each frequency band is fed into its own compressor, after which the signals are recombined at the output.

The main advantage of multi-band compression is that a loud event in one frequency band won't trigger gain reduction in the other bands. Another feature of the multiband compressor is that you are offered crossover points. This is crucial, as you are given control over where to place the frequency band. Setting these crossover points is the heart of the compressor and crucial in processing the right frequency spectrum with the right settings.

For example: if you are treating the vocals in the mid range but put your low end crossover too far into the middle range, then the low end compression settings will also affect the mid range vocals.

There is a continued debate about the merits of using multiband compression at the mastering stage but in terms of single event frequency/gain management I find it very useful. On individual sounds it can be extremely useful but on very short static (non-moving) sounds it can be redundant. So, make your compression choices based on the sound being treated and the ultimate result being aimed for.

Limiter

A limiter keeps signal peaks from exceeding a pre determined level. While a compressor reduces the overall dynamic range, a limiter affects only the highest peaks. Limiters have very fast attack times, very high compression ratios and a high threshold. You can turn your compressor into a limiter by using a very high threshold and ratio.

The 'classic' definition is that a limiter 'flattens' all peaks above a certain level, but leaves lower-level sounds intact.

Choosing the right compressor for a given task is very important not only because of the functions available but also because of the 'character' that certain compressors impart onto the sound. There are compressors that are completely transparent and do not colour the sound in any shape or form and these particular compressors are great for the more strategic tasks like mastering or overall dynamic compression for gain control. They can be used 'surgically' to reshape a sound without imparting any colouration onto the sound.

'Coloured' compressors impart a tonal character onto the sound being processed and these are extremely useful if a certain 'sound' is aimed for. I will use, for example, a Fairchild 660 mono compressor on certain drum sounds because it imparts a warm and deep colour onto the audio being processed, whereas I will use a SSL FX 384 for transparency and surgical gain management.

There are also dramatic differences between the way compressors process the audio data even though, functionally, they are processing using the same tools and settings. This comes down to the design and integration of the compressor.

I have, through time, found that certain compressors are great for certain types of tasks and with this in mind I have honed down my compressor collection to a selection of choice compressors and it will be these compressors I will use for the following examples. I have, of course, omitted hardware compressors from the working examples for obvious reasons.

The best settings to use for general audio gain management are soft and subtle settings (very low ratio values being an example) but for drum layering and reshaping tasks we can get as adventurous as we like.

Reshaping a kick drum

In the first example I am going to display how to reshape a kick drum that is already thick and full into a number of different sonic textures simply by altering the compressor's settings. The kick waveform is shown in Figure 8.3.

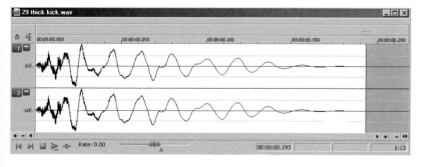

Figure 8.3
The kick waveform

Sound file

29 thick kick.wav

Figure 8.4
The compressor and its parameters

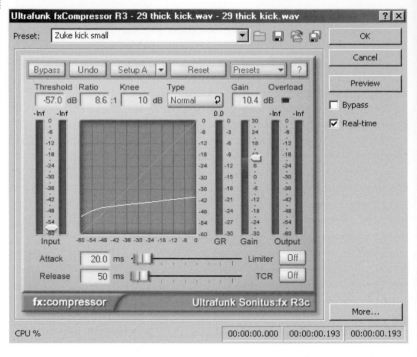

Figure 8.5
The new compressed kick waveform

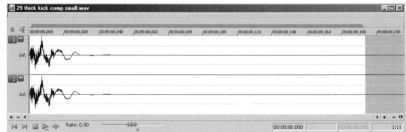

Sound file

29 thick kick comp small.wav

Figure 8.4 shows the compressor and its parameters, and Figure 8,5 the new compressed kick waveform. The new waveform is distinctly shorter and has very little body.

The important parameter values for the compressor in this example are the threshold, attack, release and ratio values, but I will also touch on the knee and gain parameters. By selecting an extremely low threshold value almost the whole input signal is made available for compression.

By selecting a 20 ms value for the attack means that 20 ms of the input signal will be uncompressed. In effect, the first 20 ms of the kick is unaffected. The compressor then acts immediately after the 20 ms 'delay'. This effectively means that the first 20 ms of the kick waveform will be louder and will punch through before the compressor acts.

By selecting a very low release value means that the gain reduction on the compressor snaps back to 0 dB before the next event starts. In this instance the kick sample is a single hit and static so the release value has little effect.

The knee value is at 10 dB which denotes it as a hard knee (lower values denote hard and higher values denote soft). In this instance a harder knee value works well for the type of sound we are after.

The gain parameter controls the amount of make-up gain to be added or subtracted from the compressed output signal. Use this to level off the compressed signal gain so that it is not too quiet or too loud that it clips.

The ratio value is around 8:1 (8.6:1). This basically means that for every 8 dB change in input level, the output changes 1 dB. For this particular example this means that everything at and beyond the attack value is compressed by a ratio of 8:1 which makes the balance of the waveform almost inaudible thus accounting for the perception of a short sample length.

In terms of drum layering this particular example would be the equivalent of creating an attack component.

Changing the tonal quality of the kick sample

In the next example I am going to completely change the tonal quality of the same kick sample and give it a much harder and harsher edge. This is particularly useful when it comes to compressing layered samples.

For this example I am going to use a different compressor as it has the right type of 'character' that I require for this particular task. Try to have a few choice compressors in your arsenal and familiarize yourself with their attributes and characteristics. Figure 8.6 shows a different compressor and its settings.

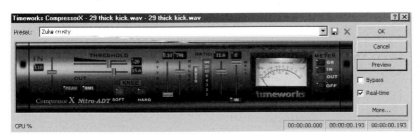

Figure 8.6
A diffferent compressor and its settings

Please note the parameter settings for this example. The distinct differences are that a soft knee setting has been selected with an immediate attack, a longer release and a higher ratio. Figure 8.7 displays the new compressed waveform.

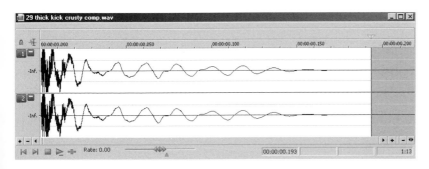

Figure 8.7
The new compressed waveform

Sound file

29 thick kick crusty comp.wav

The resultant waveform is far harsher and crispier and is now a completely new waveform ready to be used in layering projects. It is interesting to note that all that has been done is that the same kick sample has been used but compressed with different settings and the results are that we now have completely new textures to work with.

Same kick sample – a more rounded sound

The following example will deal with the same kick sample and the aim is to give a more rounded and tight sonic result. Figure 8.8 shows the new parameter settings required to achieve the above.

A great feature of this particular compressor is the graphical display at the centre of the vst.

Figure 8.8
The new parameter settings required to achieve the above

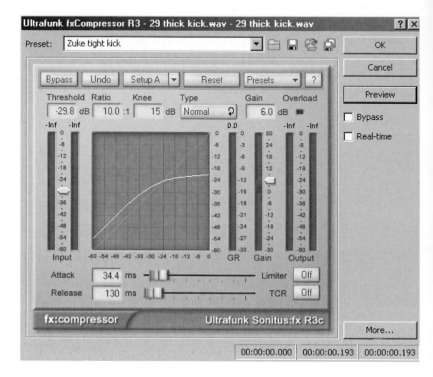

- The graph displays input level vs. output level over a 60 dB range, with grid lines placed every 6 dB in each direction.
- The input level is shown horizontally and the output level vertically. Furthermore, the graph shows a diagonal line from left to right to indicate the state where input and output levels are equal and no compression will take place.
- The bold white line displays the new shape using the compression values. This acts as a good reference tool.

Feel free to reshape the compression curve by adjusting the parameter values or by clicking with the left mouse anywhere in the graph and moving the node that appears. Figure 8.9 shows both the original and resultant waveform shapes.

These compression examples have been created to allow for the variety of results and techniques, all of which will be used later in this book when we explore 'stems'.

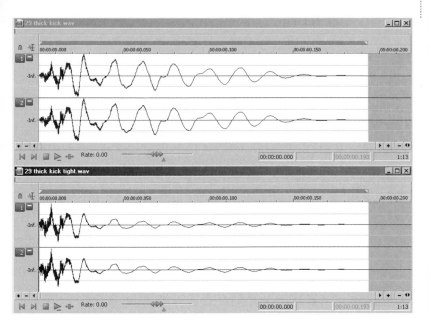

Figure 8.9
The original and resultant waveform shapes

Sound file

29 thick kick tight.wav

Using extreme settings

In the next example, I would like to demonstrate to you how to use some extreme settings to attain a 'destroyed' result. The first example deals with the same kick sample and the second example deals with a drum beat.

Figure 8.10 shows the extreme compressor settings and Figure 8.11 displays the resultant layer.

Figure 8.10
The extreme compressor settings

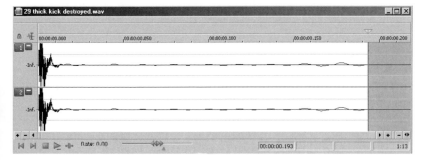

Figure 8.11
The resultant layer

Sound file

29 thick kick destroyed.wav

And now I would like to share with you how to filthy up a drum beat and give it the famous 'pumping' effect. Figure 8.12 shows the drum beat waveform and Figure 8.13 shows the extreme compressor settings.

Figure 8.12
The drum beat waveform

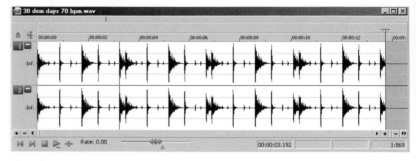

Figure 8.13
The extreme compressor settings

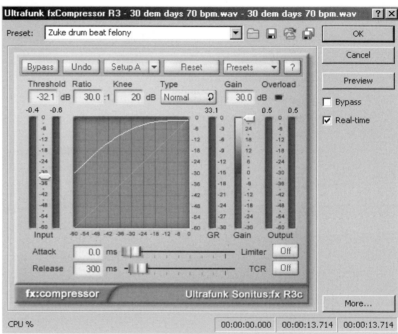

Sound file

30 dem days 70 bpm.wav

The heavy pumping effect is controlled by the release parameter. Of course, all the other parameters are important but it is the release parameter that determines how and when the compressor stops, and the attack determines when it starts again as described earlier. Figure 8.14 shows the resultant layer.

Figure 8.14
The resultant layer

Sound file

30 dem days 70 bpm pumped.wav

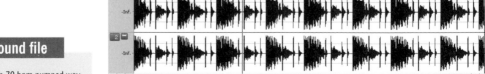

Multiband compression examples

Finally, I would like to end with a couple of multiband compression (MBC) examples. The camp is strictly divided into two factions over the merits and use of MBCs. The arguments originated, and still rage, within the mastering circles. As far as this book is concerned we are only interested in the use of MBCs for drum sounds and I believe, owing to the nature and design of the MBC, it has its uses. You need to experiment and then weigh up the pros and cons and then decide if it is a tool worth exploring.

Dynamic with MBC features

The following example makes use of a dynamic that has MBC characteristics and features. It is also regarded as a dynamic EQ and examples of this will be covered in the next chapter. Figure 8.15 shows the default settings for the MBC. Important points to note are as follows:

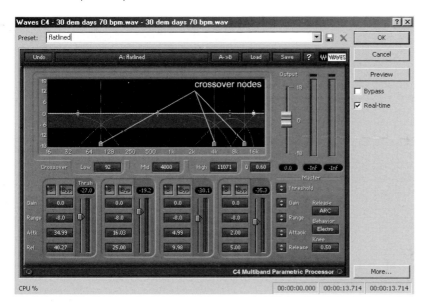

Figure 8.15
The default settings

Range

This sets the maximum gain change for a band. If set to a negative value the band is a compressor; positive values make the band into an upward or downward expander. The range also acts as a ratio control.

Crossover

To properly create a multiband compressor, a phase-compensated crossover is essential otherwise there will be undesirable artifacts and pitch shifting effects between the bands as the gains are moved independently. In addition, the crossover must have a flat frequency response when set to nominal values. All other parameters are standard and have been covered.

Figure 8.16 displays the settings I have input to alter the existing drum loop waveform.

Figure 8.16
The extreme settings

By using negative values for the ranges I have, in effect, instigated compression at each band and by using and reshaping the crossovers the movement between the bands is both distinct and fluid. Figure 8.17 shows the resultant waveform.

Figure 8.17
The resultant waveform

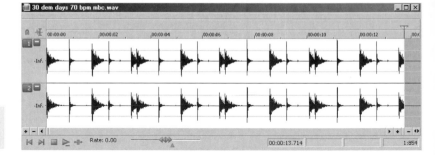

Sound file

30 dem days 70 bpm mbc.wav

Extreme settings

The final MBC example entails extreme settings. I have done this so that you can see and hear how much control an MBC can offer if designed and integrated properly.

As you can hear almost the whole of the snare sound has been removed, along with the harshness and attack of the kick and the attack and body of the hi hat, and this is clearly evident by looking at Figure 8.18. Even the pan position of the hi hat has been altered and the kick is now very woolly and deep. In my view MBC has a place in the 'dynamic tools' closet and as with any tool it has its uses.

Figure 8.18
The extreme settings

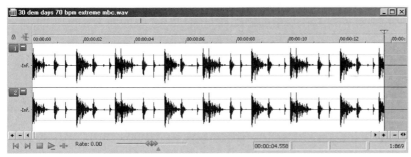

Figure 8.19
The resultant waveform

Sound file

30 dem days 70 bpm extreme
mbc.wav

I hope this chapter has gone some way in demystifying how the compressor works and what results can be achieved with it. The compressor is without a doubt one of the most important of the dynamic tools available. It is not only a dynamic gain control tool but a wonderful sonic sculptor. Use it but know how to use it and the sound design world starts to look a little less daunting.

Dynamics: equalization

Info

Sound Equalization Tips and Tricks is available from the publisher of this book.

I have written a book on this subject entitled *Sound Equalization Tips and Tricks* and therefore do not want to go into too much detail here by repeating the content. However, a condensed and more focused chapter on this subject relative to drum layering and processing is important.

To define what equalization (EQ) is would take quite a while but a condensed definition would be:

A dynamic processor which uses filters to alter the balance of frequencies in a sound.

This is achieved by using a number of filter circuits, which apply positive or negative gain to selected frequency ranges. The positive gain is referred to as 'boost' and the negative gain is referred to as 'cut'. This is as simple as you can get. In fact, this definition has helped me considerably and particularly when I was a beginner.

There are two types of EQ and both are relevant when it comes to drum processing: Corrective Equalization and Creative Equalization. Let me briefly explain what each one is.

Corrective equalization

This form of EQ is used to correct any anomalies that may exist in a sound (removing noise, rumble etc, and abating problematic frequencies, compensating for room inaccuracies etc). However, precision EQ tasks will require corrective methods as opposed to creative ones.

A good example of this would be to use corrective EQ to separate frequencies in a mix. Corrective EQ is also used at the mastering stage to compensate and accommodate frequencies that would otherwise render the master as 'unacceptable'. In other words the mastering engineer (ME) will use corrective EQ to create a master suitable for the desired medium. Of course, creative EQ techniques also play a part but first and foremost the master must be as 'correct' as possible with consideration for the entire frequency spectrum of the master. The same applies when processing individual sounds.

In terms of processing drums sounds corrective EQ could be used to remove any anomalies like noise, glitches etc. It could also be used to resolve problematic frequencies like clashes or masking when layering.

Creative equalization

This form of EQ is used to 'colour' a sound or to reshape its characteristics to create a new sonic template (boosting the mid-range frequencies of a kick drum to accent the punch and body is a good example).

Both forms of EQ are important when it comes to drum processing and layering and a brief understanding of the functions and controls is very important. With this in mind please digest the following as the ensuing examples require that you are familiar with the terminologies and processes.

Cut-off frequency

This is the point (frequency) at which the filter begins to filter (block or cut out). The filter will lower the volume of the frequencies above or below the cut-off frequency depending on the type of filter used.

Attenuation

This 'lowering of the volume of the frequencies,' is called attenuation. In the case of a low-pass filter, the frequencies above the cut-off are attenuated. In the case of a hi-pass filter, the frequencies below the cut-off are attenuated.

Resonance

Boosting the narrow band of frequencies at the cut-off point is called resonance. Also known as Q and bandwidth, in effect, the higher the resonance, the narrower the bandwidth. Figure 9.1 displays the relative parameters for resonance and cut-off.

Figure 9.1
The relative parameters for resonance and cut-off

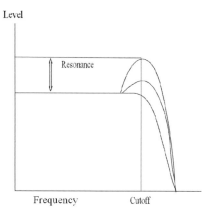

Cut

To reduce the level of a signal using a filter. To lower the frequency amplitude of a band.

Q

Also known as 'width of the filter response', this is the 'centre frequency' of the bandwidth and is measured in Hz. Also know as bandwidth and resonance. A high Q value denotes a narrow filter width (bandwidth). A low Q value denotes a wide filter width (bandwidth).

This is actually a very important piece of information because with the Q control alone you can make your audio sound high and brittle or warm and musical. This does not mean that you must use low Q values all the time, in the hope of attaining warmth, but you must understand what frequencies need filtering. If your intent is to use EQ as a musical tool, then be aware of what the Q value can do to audio. For creative EQ, this is a weapon often ignored.

Slope
The rate at which a high or low frequency EQ section reduces the level above or below the cut-off frequency is termed as the 'Slope' and the shape and parameters are denoted as dB per octave and are usually: 6, 12, 18 or 24dB/octave.
Slope also determines the characteristic of the filter and can range from smooth to extreme (gentle to aggressive).

Boost
To apply gain or to increase by level. Measured in dB.

Band
A single filter in an equalizer or a range of pre-determined frequencies.

Centre frequency
The frequency at which a peaking filter applies maximum gain.

Filter
A circuit which alters the level of a limited range of frequencies.

Filter shapes

Bell
An EQ with a peak in its response denoted by its shape and quite common nowadays on most virtual EQs. The bell shape has symmetrical response characteristics. In other words it has the same response whether boosting or cutting.

Shelf
A high or low frequency EQ where the response extends from the selected frequency to the highest or lowest frequency values in the audio range.

Low-pass and high-pass
A low-pass shelving filter passes all frequencies below its cut-off frequency, but attenuates all frequencies above its cut-off frequency. Similarly, a high-pass filter passes all frequencies above its cut-off frequency, but affects all frequencies below its cut-off frequency.

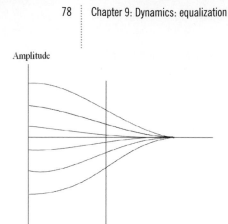
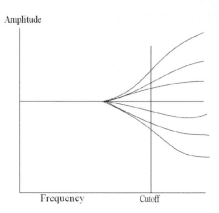

Figures 9.2 and 9.3
Low pass and high pass filters

As Figures 9.2 and 9.3 show; in the low-pass filter diagram the frequencies below the cut-off are allowed to pass through whereas the frequencies above the cut-off are attenuated.

In the hi-pass filter diagram the frequencies below the cut-off are attenuated and the frequencies above the cut-off are allowed to pass through.

Parametric

Invented by George Massenberg, this filter is one of the most commonly used today. This filter controls three parameters, frequency, bandwidth and gain. You select the range of frequencies you want to boost or cut, you select the width of that range and use the gain to boost or cut the frequencies, within the selected bandwidth, by a selected amount.

The frequencies not in the bandwidth are not altered. If you widen the bandwidth to the limit of the upper and lower frequencies ranges then this is called shelving. Most parametric filters have shelving parameters.

Figure 9.4
A parametric EQ

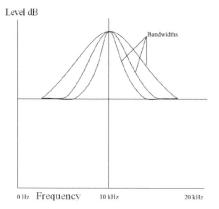

Parametric filters are great for more complex filtering jobs and can be used to create real dynamic effects because they can attenuate or boost any range of frequencies. Basically, the parametric EQ places several active filters across the frequency spectrum. Each filter is designated to a frequency range, low, mid, high etc. You have the usual cut/boost, resonant frequency and bandwidth. It is these qualities and the control over them that places this particular EQ in the producer's arsenal of dynamic tools. However, you need to understand what you are doing when using a parametric EQ, otherwise things can go very wrong.

There are many more filter types and they are all covered in my book mentioned earlier. For the sake of this book I have only covered the basic EQs that we will use for drum layering projects.

Let us now explore some of the characteristics and features of the EQs mentioned above and use them in working examples.

A bright acoustic kick drum sample

The following example entails taking a bright acoustic kick drum sample and processing it with EQ to create a much lower and deeper resultant layer (Figure 9.5).

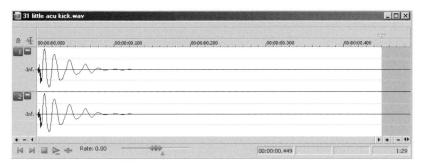

Figure 9.5
A basic acoustic kick drum waveform

Sound file

31 little acu kick.wav

I have chosen a nice 2 band EQ to start with as we are dealing with a short and static waveform that does not need a great many bands. Figure 9.6 shows the 2 band EQ and its parameters.

The two nodes you see in the display are the two bands. They can be moved by using the mouse and dragging the nodes to the desired positions or by inputting values via the parameter controls. Nodes/bands can be 'switched' on or off. This allows you to work with one or more bands.

Figure 9.6
The 2 band EQ and its parameters

Figure 9.7
The settings

Gain, frequency and Q have all been covered as have the 'shapes' in the band drop down menu. Figure 9.7 shows the settings I have created to use for the process.

Selecting the right EQ curve/shape for each band is crucial as this determines how the EQ behaves and what sonic texture it imparts. For band 1 I have selected the bell shape for the filter response as I do not want to apply any hi or low shelving at the sample start. The bell shape also allows for a more gradual rise and drop for the peak, being asymmetrical in that it has symmetrical response characteristics irrespective of whether I cut or boost. I have instigated a 7.7 dB boost at 69 Hz. For band 2 I have selected a low-pass shape and instigated a huge cut at 269 Hz.

Figure 9.8
The new resultant layer

Sound file

31 little acu kick low boost.wav

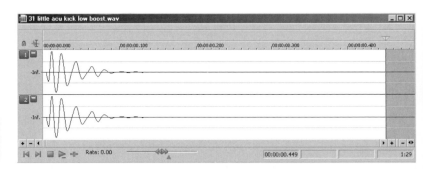

Emphasizing the second band

In the next example I have placed emphasis on the second band using a hi-pass shape so that the resultant layer will sound mid to high frequency rich with very little in terms of low frequency content. What I suggest is that you toggle between the hi-shelf, low-pass and bell shapes and assess the huge differences in sonic character. Figure 9.9 shows the parameter settings and Figure 9.10 shows the resultant layer.

These two examples display how easy it is to create new sonic textures using only 2 bands of an EQ. You could use just a single band if you want

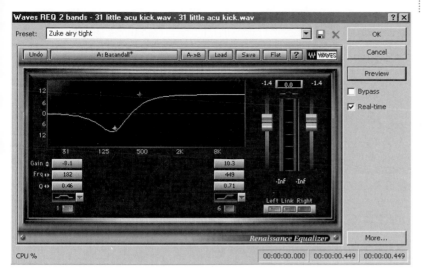

Figure 9.9
The parameter settings

but I like to have at least 2 bands to play with as this allows me more control over the response.

An important point to make when using any form of EQ for boosting or cutting is that you need to compensate for the boosts and cuts using the main output gain controls so that files do not clip or sound too quiet. Basically, much like the compression examples, the main output gain control acts as a compensation tool.

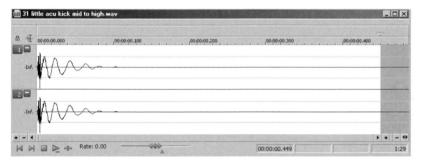

Figure 9.10
The resultant layer

Sound file

31 little acu kick mid to high.wav

It is an undeniable truth that the more bands you have to play with the more detailed the processing. But at what point does one decide how many bands to use for a given task? I like to think of bands as simply ranges of frequencies and the desired result determines how many bands are needed. The simplest answer is to use the most potent weapons/tools at your disposal: your ears.

In the next example I am going to use 4 bands and for a specific reason. I want to be able to shape a sound in detail taking into account the entire frequency spectrum. The result I am after will become evident once the settings are seen.

Boosting the low and high frequencies

I am using the same kick example and this time I am trying to achieve a warm yet clear result with expression for the mid to high frequencies. In effect, I am trying to 'hollow' out the low-mid to mid frequencies leaving, and boosting, the low and high frequencies.

The vst I am using acts as both a multiband compressor (MBC) and a dynamic equalizer and this particular dynamic has been covered in the previous chapter. The reason I have chosen this specific processor is that it has crossover points and a range function which acts as either a compressor or expander depending on the values selected (Figure 9.11).

Figure 9.11

The settings of the processor

Bands 2 and 3 have undergone cuts and bands 1 and 4 have been boosted. The crossovers have been adjusted for a smooth transition between the bands and the ranges have been kept constant with negative values to allow for compression. The attack and release values have wide variations and the master output gain has been adjusted to compensate for the gains. Figure 9.12 shows the resultant layer. Although the resultant layer sounds markedly different to the original, what is interesting to note is the shape of the new waveform compared to the original. They look very similar in terms of their ADSRs but exhibit different tonal characteristics.

Figure 9.12

The resultant layer

Sound file

31 little acu kick hollow.wav

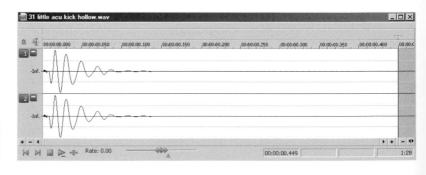

For the next example I would like to use a graphic equalizer. It strikes me as quite strange that very few people seem to use graphic equalizers in the studio. They are potent tools and are not restricted to hi-fi use.

Graphic equalizer

A graphic equalizer is simply a set of filters, each with a fixed centre frequency that cannot be changed. The only control you have is the amount of boost or cut in each frequency band. This boost or cut is most often controlled with sliders. The sliders are a graphic representation of the frequency response, hence the name 'graphic' equalizer.

The more frequency bands you have, the more control and accuracy you have over the frequency response. A graphic equalizer (Figure 9.13) uses a set of band-pass filters that are designed to completely isolate certain frequency bands.

Figure 9.13
A graphic equalizer

Figure 9.14 shows the frequency response of a band-pass filter. A filter that passes frequencies between two limits is known as a band-pass filter. This filter attenuates frequencies below and above the cut-off and leaves the frequencies at the cut-off. It is, in effect, a low-pass and a hi-pass together.

The advantage of this filter is that you can eliminate the lower and higher frequencies and be left with a band of frequencies that you can then use for isolating a narrow band of frequencies.

What I like about this particular graphic EQ is that it is a little more detailed than your average graphic EQ. Most graphic EQs provide slider controls for each band and not much else, but this particular vst

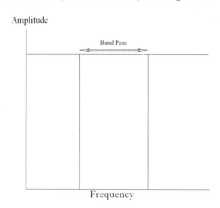

Figure 9.14
Frequency response of a band-pass filter

provides bandwidth control and comes with a limiter. Providing 15 sliders that control cuts (-24 dB) and boosts (+24 dB) for a range of frequencies from 40 Hz to 16 kHz, this EQ allows for multi band control over a signal.

For this particular example I am going to use the graphic EQ to create simple yet new sonic textures and the first texture I am going to create is that of a pseudo band pass.

Creating a pseudo band pass

Figure 9.15 shows the ballpark settings for a pseudo band pass using only fixed bands. Although this is not a true band pass (pseudo) it does display how the same effect can be mimicked by attenuating the low and hi frequencies to leave only the middle frequencies. This is the equivalent of the 'telephone' effect (narrow mid banded). The new waveform (Figure 9.16) clearly displays the low and high frequency attenuations.

Figure 9.15

Ballpark settings for a pseudo band pass using only fixed bands

Figure 9.16

The new waveform

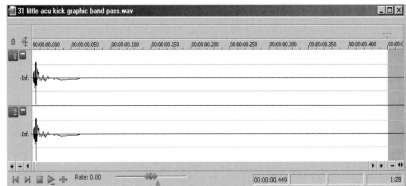

Sound file

31 little acu kick graphic band pass.wav

Attenuating the mid range frequencies

In the next example I am going to attenuate the mid range frequencies and boost the low and high frequencies. Figure 9.17 shows the extreme graphic EQ settings.

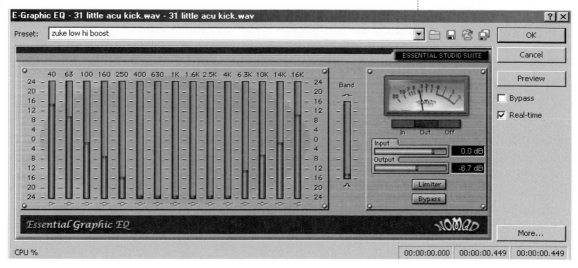

Figure 9.17
The extreme graphic EQ settings

The boosts at the low frequencies are self explanatory but boosts at the higher frequencies and particularly at 16 kHz might seem like madness as it might be safe to assume that this kick waveform does not enter that frequency domain. However, the 14-16 kHz frequency range is usually denoted as the 'air band' and this allows for presence. Figure 9.18 displays the resultant waveform.

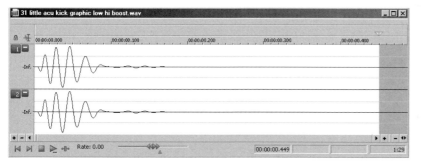

Figure 9.18
The resultant waveform

Sound file

31 little acu kick graphic low hi boost.wav

The graphic EQ is a dynamic that must not be ignored simply because of its fixed band nature. This allows for a different and more detailed type of control.

By familiarizing yourself with the differences in both features and results with the varying forms of EQ you will be in a strong position to make instinctual decisions as to which to use for any given task.

Creative EQ

Adding subtle warmth

For the final few examples I would like to concentrate on creative EQ and particularly that of imparting 'colour' onto a signal.

I have a number of hardware and software EQs that I use for this particular type of equalization but one that I generally 'go to' for adding subtle warmth is Nomad Factory's Retrology series and particularly the Motown which is a '7 band passive EQ emulation of the hardware equivalent used by Motown engineers' (quote from Nomad). This EQ is as simple as they get.

Figure 9.19
The EQ and its selected settings

Figure 9.20
The resultant waveform

Sound file

31 little acu kick motown.wav

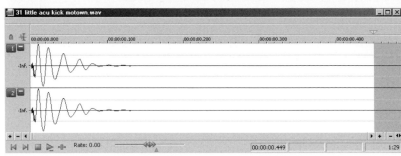

Figure 9.19 shows the EQ and its selected settings. The settings above are quite subtle with no extreme boosting at any of the frequencies. Figure 9.20 displays the resultant waveform. The result is a smooth and more spacious sonic texture with a 'rounded' feel to it.

Adding a low punch to the kick

The next example reshapes the waveform to exhibit a low punch but still maintain a warm edge to the sound. Figure 9.21 displays the new settings for the Motown. The parameter settings are not extremes as far as drum processing goes, but there are distinct boosts and cuts which account for the punch element. As with all EQ projects compensating at the output stage is essential and this can be seen above. Figure 9.22 displays the resultant waveform.

Figure 9.21
The new settings for the Motown

Figure 9.22
The resultant waveform

Sound file

31 little acu kick motown warm punch.wav

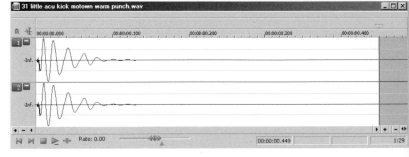

This waveform now sounds fuller and still rounded with a distinct punch at the lower to lo-mid frequencies.

I would like to end this chapter with a snare example.

Adding colouration to a snare

In this instance I have chosen an electro snare and the goal is to allow for colouration around the entire frequency spectrum. The aim is to give the snare a fuller and deeper texture without losing the top end (higher frequencies). The settings I have chosen reflect this. Figure 9.23 shows the unaffected (dry) snare waveform.

Figure 9.23
The unaffected (dry) snare waveform

Sound file

32 electro snare.wav

Although I could use any EQ to boost and cut certain frequencies to attain a deeper resultant waveform I have chosen to stick with the coloured EQ as I want to impart the characteristics of the EQ onto the sound itself. Figure 9.24 displays the settings chosen for the EQ.

Figure 9.24
The settings chosen for the EQ

Almost all the bands have been boosted with the exception of the 12.5 kHz which has been cut. This has allowed for the brighter top end to be abated so that the existing frequencies can shine through. Figure 9.25 shows the resultant waveform.

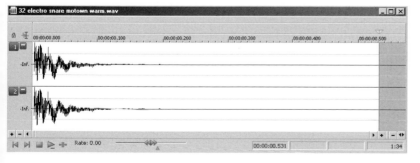

Figure 9.25
The resultant waveform

Sound file

32 electro snare motown warm.wav

Info

Sound Equalization Tips and Tricks is available from the publisher of this book.

Equalization is a vast topic and one that merits deep study. In terms of using corrective or creative EQ the best way forward is simply to experiment. In this chapter I have deliberately stayed away from conducting too many corrective EQ examples as this will be covered in the next chapter when dealing with creating frequency spaces for layering projects. In terms of removing problematic frequencies, glitches noise etc I have covered this in depth in my *Sound Equalization Tips and Tricks* book.

I hope this chapter has gone some way in explaining how to apply EQ to a sound and what the benefits are. As with all the chapters in this book, please experiment until you have a clear understanding of the techniques used and the results attained.

Stems and tree

This chapter is not as complicated as it may seem. The 'tree' system is one that has already been covered in Chapter 1 'Structure'.

As with all layering projects there is a hierarchical system whereby the layers, when combined, go to form the resultant/objective sound. Whether the layers are ADSR components, entire and complete waveforms or tones, the layering process is the same every time.

However, there is another method for layering sounds and that entails using multi channels/tracks for all the layers and mixing the channels as if they formed a song. Each layer would be consigned to an audio channel, or triggered via midi, in the sequencing software or DAW. This 'multi tracking' system works extremely well as each channel can be further processed independently of other channels with a final tier of processing for the main master stereo output/file, and this makes for an extremely versatile system.

Each one of the midi/audio channels (layers) will then have a 'stem' that leads to a form of processing. Think of these stems as branches. Figure 10.1 outlines the relationships between the layers and stems within a tree context.

Definition

Tree: a model for organizing a database in a hierarchal arrangement.

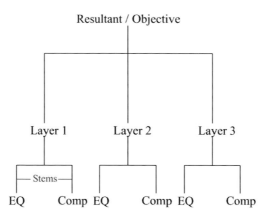

Figure 10.1
The tree and stem concept in graphical form

I have constructed a very simple tree system whereby each layer has 2 stems and each stem leads to a form of dynamic processing, in this instance EQ and compression.

In reality each stem could be an inserted effect/dynamic within the same audio channel. This may seem confusing as the stem looks like a physical entity designated to a process, but it is actually the processes that account

for the number of stems. In other words each stage of processing is regarded as a stem. This makes explaining what happens to a layer, in terms of processing, much simpler.

This process allows for extreme flexibility with the source signal remaining
intact whilst processing is applied. If the processing result is not to the user's
liking then the process can be removed or altered without having a destructive outcome. Destructive simply means that the process cannot be reversed
or 'undone'. Additionally, because channels are used in a multi tracking mix
situation then they can be 'grouped' into group channels whereby additional
stems can be applied to the group channel. This allows for processing more
than one sound at a time.

I use Cubase SX as my DAW and all the ensuing examples will be per-
formed using that particular piece of software. Please use the information
provided, and migrate it across to your sequencing/editing software. The
principles and techniques are the same.

I will start with midi triggered examples but the same methodology applies
to imported audio files. Initially, the idea is to set up an environment within
the DAW that is easy to work with, uncluttered and sensibly labeled. As mentioned earlier I am pedantic and old school in my approach to working
through projects. I like to label everything and create a sensible hierarchical
system that is both easy to understand and simple to access.

In terms of creating a project within Cubase I have deliberately started
with a blank template. I have added 3 instances of midi channels. I have
named each one dependent on what I will be triggering within that channel
(kick1, kick2 and kick3). I have then streamlined the whole template page
(environment) to display only what is relevant for this project, and for ease
of use I have colour coded each channel so as to provide a visual reference
when trying to navigate through the different menu pages.

For the sake of simplicity, and for your reference, I have enclosed an
image of the environment (Figure 10.2) and have supplied a brief explanation of the layout.

I have created three midi channels and loaded three instances of a drum
vsti called Battery 3 in each midi channel. I have named each midi channel
relevant to the project; in this case Kick1: midi channel 1, Kick2: midi channel 2 and Kick3: midi channel 3. I have colour coded each midi channel for
ease of referencing. I have streamlined the whole arrange page (environment) to only show tools and features that I may need. Everything else that
is of little use has been removed. This allows for a simple and uncluttered
template.

The default template I have created above is also reflected within the
mixer page in Cubase (Figure 10.3). The mixer page displays the three midi
channels and three instrument channels, along with the stereo in and stereo
out channels. The stereo out channel is the main stereo out of the DAW and
further effects and dynamics can be inserted here if required.

By clicking on the 'e' on any channel allows me to edit the channel settings. It is here that we will insert effects and dynamics during the following
examples.

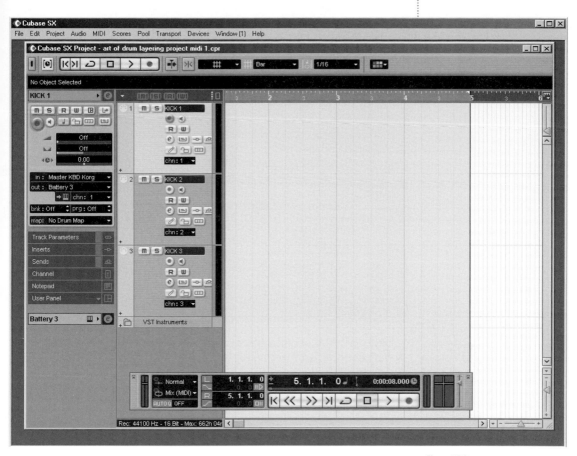

Battery 3 is a very simple vsti and I have trimmed the default template to display only the basic cells where I drag samples to from the different folder locations (accessible via the Browser tool).

Each cell is triggered via midi and in this instance cell A1 is triggered as C1 on a keyboard or midi controller.

Figure 10.2
The main default template within Cubase for this layering project

Figure 10.3
The streamlined mixer window in Cubase

Figure 10.4
The browser at the lower half of the vsti

Figure 10.4 shows the browser at the lower half of the vsti with the high-lighted cell showing where I have dragged the sample to the browser.

The dragging of samples from a defined location and dropping into select-ed cells makes this particular vsti a great tool for auditioning samples prior to using them and for placing them into the relevant midi trigger assigns.

The next step is to select another kick sound within the next instance of Battery 3 and again to repeat this for the final kick sound. In Cubase I have cre-ated a simple pattern of kick triggers on each bar of a song that is running at 120 bpm tempo. I have repeated (copy/paste) the same midi pattern for each of the 3 midi channels. This allows the kicks to all be played at the same time on each bar. Figure 10.5 shows the new midi pattern song for the drum sounds. The following three drum sounds are being used in this project via Battery 3:

Figure 10.5
The new midi pattern song for the drum sounds

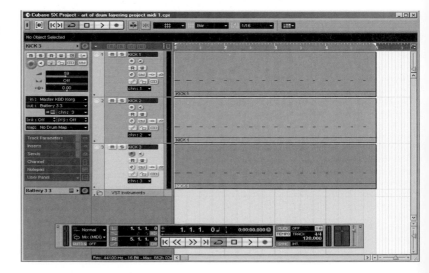

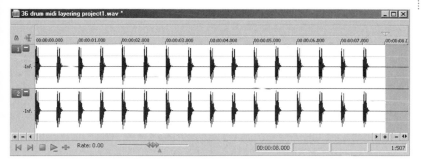

Figure 10.6
The audio file for all three kicks played together

Sound file

36 drum midi layering project1.wav

Midi channel 1: 33 kik005 sweet.wav
Midi channel 2: 34 kik006 sweet as.wav
Midi channel 3: 35 kik010 magic muff.wav

Figure 10.7
The level fader on the side for a selected channel

Figure 10.6 shows the audio file for all three kicks played together. The first, and most basic, tool available within Cubase is simply the channel fader tool that controls the gain of the channel. This allows for instant control of level changes for each channel from the main arrange window. Figure 10.7 shows the channel gain fader for midi channel 3. By using the faders for each midi channel the task of varying volumes (gains) for each channel becomes easy as it is both instant and visual. For finer and more detailed editing involving effects and dynamics it is best to access the mixer page and edit within the instrument channel.

As detailed earlier please leave ample headroom on each channel so that when we start to use dynamics, particularly when boosting, the main stereo output does not clip. In fact, make sure none of the instrument/midi channels clips either as all gains will be summed at the output stage.

Figure 10.8 displays the metering for each channel and the master output bus within the mixer page.

Figure 10.8
The metering for each channel and the master output bus

It is at this stage that we can conduct further processing. By selecting (clicking on) the letter 'e' on the channel you will access the channel edit settings. I am going to work on Kick 1 by shaping an EQ curve and then inserting a compressor on the channel.

To work with any one file it is best to isolate the sound by using the 'solo' function, editing the sound and then A/B this with the un-soloed version. This allows for hearing the sound in isolation when soloed, and then referencing with the other two sounds when solo has been deselected.

Figure 10.9
The 'channel edit' page

Figure 10.9 shows the channel edit page and you can see the EQ curve I have created, along with an instance of compression that has been inserted into the channel although not yet activated.

Figure 10.10
Compressor settings

Figure 10.10 shows the compressor and its settings for Kick1, and Figure 10.11 displays the rendered audio file for Kick1. '37 kick1 eq and comp.wav' is the rendered audio file with the EQ and compression:

You will notice that I have left ample headroom so that this file, when

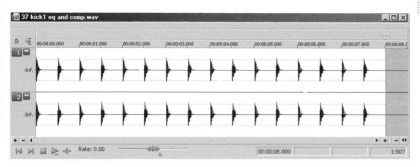

Figure 10.11
The rendered audio file for Kick1

Sound file

37 kick1 eq and comp.wav

summed with the other two sounds, will not clip the master stereo bus output. Short of going through each channel setting, one at a time, I have set up the mixer page to display the EQ curves for each Kick midi instrument channel (Figure 10.12).

The EQ curves for each kick in the mixer page are shown in Figure 10.12.

Figure 10.12
The EQ curves for each kick

Sound file

38 3 kicks eq.wav

The EQ values and curves are displayed which makes fine tuning the individual channels really easy.

Kick 1 has had boosts at 186 Hz (3.8 dB) and 7.1 kHz (4.5 dB)
Kick 2 has a boost at 738 Hz (7.7 dB) and a huge cut at 7.38 kHz (-10.7 dB)
Kick 3 has had a prominent boost at 100 Hz (6.0 dB)

We have already seen the values for the compressor's settings for Kick 1. Now let us look at the settings for Kicks 2 and 3. Please note that the same compressor is being used for all the kicks. This is for simplicity's sake.

Figure 10.13 displays the Kick 2 compressor with its settings, and Figure 10.14 displays the Kick 3 compressor with its settings.

Figure 10.13
The Kick 2 compressor with its settings

Figure 10.14
The Kick 3 compressor with its settings

Sound file

39 3 kicks eq and comp.wav

Listen to the rendered file that encompasses all three Kicks with their EQ and compressor settings.

In the above examples I have used compression to shape the dynamics for added colour as opposed to aiming for max volume. With this in mind it is often quite common for people to include another global compressor across the main stereo output bus to then boost the final signal. I have done exactly this (Figure 10.15) but have used a multiband compressor so I can fine tune the frequency bands with separate settings. Figure 10.15 shows the global compressor settings and Figure 10.16 the rendered master file.

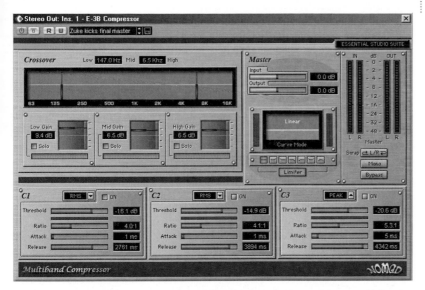

Figure 10.15
Global compressor settings

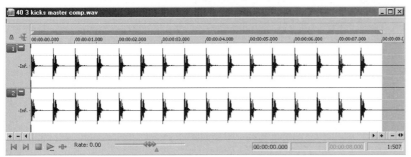

Figure 10.16
The rendered master file

Sound file

40 3 kicks master comp.wav

If you listen to the final rendered file you will notice that the MBC (multi-band compressor) has added more punch and afforded a nice tail which sounds 'pumped' (the breathing effect mentioned earlier).

As I mentioned earlier in this chapter the same approach is used whether working with midi or imported audio files. The only distinction is that, instead of creating midi channels for the sounds, you need to create audio channels and then import the audio files to their respective channels. The processing afterwards is exactly the same as if dealing with midi instrument channels.

Using stems for layers in a DAW environment is extremely flexible, as you have seen, but the stems do not end at single processes inserted on a channel. One of the most useful, and flexible, techniques is to create a group channel and then to send individual channels to the created group channel and then to apply effects/dynamics. This, in effect, is akin to sub mixing.

Group processing

Once I have processed my layers I will often take a stem to a group and apply additional processing there. The advantage of creating a group channel is that I can send any number of channels, be they midi instrument or audio, to the group channel and apply a single or multi process to all the signals simultaneously.

Using the current project I am going to show you how to create a group channel and then to send channels to the group. To work cleanly for this particular example I am going to disable the master stereo bus compressor (MBC) and then to enable it later once the group channel has undergone the necessary processing.

Figure 10.17 shows the menu options required to create a group channel and Figure 10.18 shows the created group channel below the last midi channel. Be sure to name the group channel as you may need, at a future date, to create more group channels. I have named this particular group channel 'Drum Processing'. The group channel will be visible in the mixer page exactly the same as all the other created channels.

Figure 10.17
The menu options required to create a group channel

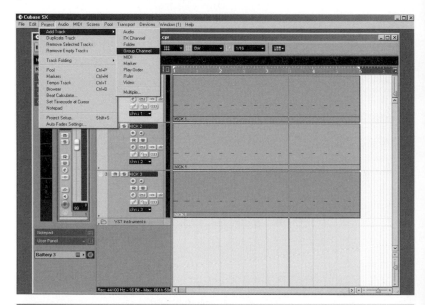

Figure 10.18
The created group channel below the last midi channel

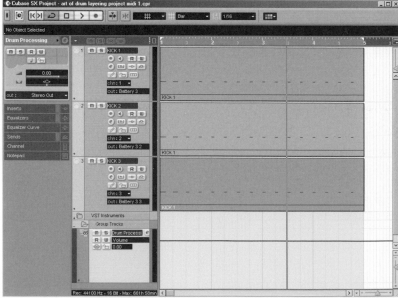

We now need to send individual channels to the group channel and enable each channel and set the amount of the signal that we want sent there. For simplicity's sake I have already sent Kick 1 channel to the group channel 'Drum Processing' and have set the amount of the send signal to maximum (Figure 10.19).

Figure 10.19
How to send a channel to a group channel

After we perform the same procedure for all the Kick channels, we can then go to the group channel in the mixer page and select and insert an effect or dynamic in the group channel. I have selected the Quad Frohmage filter and I have chosen this just to show you how extreme we can go with all the three layers. Figure 10.20 displays the group channel with the inserted dynamic Quad Frohmage.

Figure 10.20
The group channel with the inserted dynamic Quad Frohmage

Figure 10.21
The Quad Frohmage settings

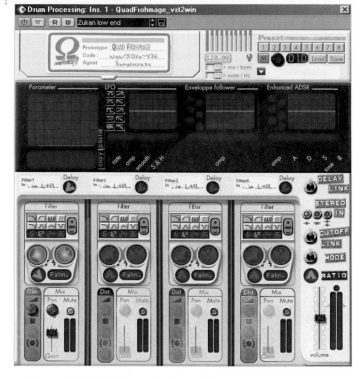

Figure 10.21 displays the Quad Frohmage settings. I must say, I love this particular filter as it is manic but it can also be used to create subtle textures.

Now that we have sent all the three Kick channels to the group and edited the dynamic to taste, we can now go back to the master stereo bus channel and reshape the compressor to accommodate the dynamics of the new texture. Figure 10.22 shows the new master compressor settings.

Figure 10.22
The new master compressor settings

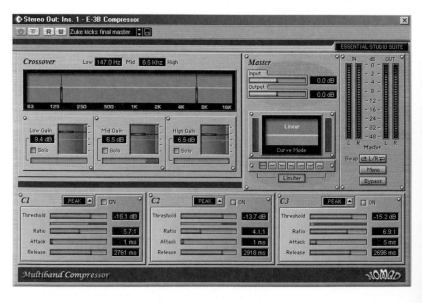

Parallel compression

In the next example I will be using a technique that many of you have heard of: parallel compression or NY (New York) Compression.

The process is extremely simple and entails using two channels, one with a compressor inserted in the channel and set to completely 'wet' (affected) and the other running the dry unaffected version of the same piece of audio that needs affecting. In essence, you make a copy of the audio you want to treat and use a compressor on the copied version and fully wet, and then mix this affected (wet) version with the untreated and dry original version.

The best technique is to use the bus out or aux on the channel to send the audio to the compressor and feed its output back into another channel. However, using the 'copy' technique and affecting the copy on a separate channel and mixing to taste also works.

The beauty of using parallel compression over a simple compressor on an insert on a channel is that you have far more dynamic control over the 'wet' and 'dry' signals. The dry channel maintains the dynamics of the unprocessed audio, and the compressed channel offers colour and body. Mixing the two affords endless variations of dynamic shaping.

In this example instead of using midi channels we will use audio channels. The technique and procedure are exactly the same as those using midi channels. Figure 10.23 displays the new arrange template.

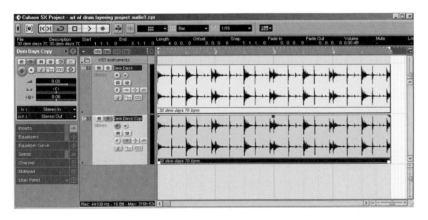

Figure 10.23
The new arrange template

Sound file

43 dem days 70 bpm.wav

In this instance I have created two stereo audio channels. I have imported the audio file twice with the second audio channel being an exact copy of the first. The mixer page is shown in Figure 10.24.

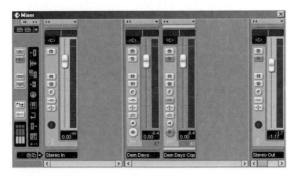

Figure 10.24
The mixer page

I have separated the relevant channels so as not to clutter the screen and to make it easy for you to follow the layout. In the copied channel I am going to insert a compressor. Please take note of the settings as I have created very extreme settings so as to attain the 'pumping or breathing' effect. Figure 10.25 shows the extreme settings I have created for the 'pump/breathing' effect.

Figure 10.25
The extreme settings

Sound file

44 audio pump eff comp.wav

Listen to the audio file and you will hear that the heavy 'pumping' effect is clearly audible and it is this effect that will be used in parallel with the untreated original version. They will then be mixed to taste and further treatment can be applied at any point on any channel. Figure 10.26 shows the mixer page with both channels active.

Figure 10.26
The mixer page

Sound file

45 final parallel audio comp.wav

This technique is not limited to single channels and can be applied to group channels as well. You may have more than one channel that you want to run a copy of with compression affected on the copied channel and so long as you want the same compressor settings on the copies it makes sense to send those channels to a group channel and apply the compressor on that channel. Additionally, you can create a number of group channels and apply different compressors and compressor settings to the channels for variety. In fact, you can apply any number of effects or dynamics to any or all channels.

It is endless what you can do with this form of editing and processing in a multi track situation.

Using the copy technique

Finally, I would like to end with an example of drum beat layering using the copy technique to add variety and colour.

To be successful in determining what effect and dynamic to apply to a copied layer it is helpful if you have an idea of what the end result should sound like, much like layering single shot drum sounds. However, the beauty of treating copied layers is that even if you have no idea of what the resultant layer will sound like it is great fun just experimenting.

I am going to use the same drum beat that we used in the previous example and use the same copy technique but this time I am going to use a filter and a reverb on the copied audio channel and mix this 'wet' (treated) version with the original dry beat, much as we did in the parallel compression example, and create a new texture.

Using the same template as the parallel compression example but without the compressor I am going to insert a filter and reverb in the channel. Figure 10.27 shows the filter and reverb inserts and Figure 10.28 displays the filter and its parameter settings.

Figure 10.27
The filter and reverb inserts

Figure 10.28
The filter and its parameter settings

By using the filter I am able to reshape the drum beat to exhibit a nice rounded squelchy sound simply by using the right cut-off and resonance values and then triggering this with a synced pulse shaped with the 'feel' in mind. Please feel free to experiment with varying values and enjoy the results. This will help attune your ears/brain.

Figure 10.29 shows the reverb and its parameter settings. The filter and reverb together sounds spacious and very coloured, and please note that I have left ample headroom in the audio file to allow for any further processing.

Figure 10.29
The reverb and its parameter settings

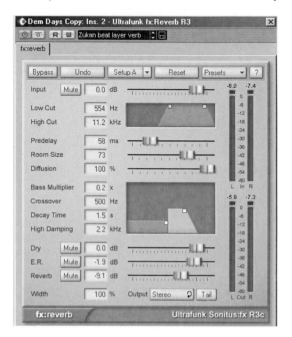

Sound file

47 filter and reverb layer beat.wav

The final step is to mix the 'wet' (treated copy) version with the original dry version. Experiment with gain changes until you are satisfied with the outcome. Pay particular attention to the gain balances between the kick and snare so that there is no gain bias towards either. Figure 10.30 displays the mixer page.

Figure 10.30
The mixer page

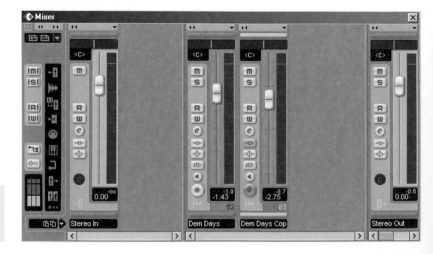

Sound file

48 final beat layer filter and reverb.wav

You will notice from Figure 10.30 that I have disabled the compressor on the master output bus. I have done this so that you can hear the summed dry and wet files uncoloured and reshaped by the compressor.

The stems and tree technique is a very simple way of arranging the hierarchy of your project. Not only does it allow for a clear and concise way of ordering tasks but it also provides a visual reference for the project requirements. I will often draw the tree and stems and plan which effects and dynamics need to be used. Of course, this can change at any point, even during a project, but the process of thinking a project through and writing down the tools necessary ingrains the whole process into memory and makes future workflows far easier to navigate.

The examples outlined in this chapter are apt for both audio and midi channels. The difference between the two, in terms of ease, is the fact that when dealing with audio the waveform editing can be applied within the DAW's generic audio editor. Midi also has a lot of editing tools available but they are different in nature to audio editing tools. For example: creating ADSR templates from a waveform in the DAW's audio editor after importing cannot be truthfully replicated using midi. So, it all comes down to the project requirements and how you, the individual, like to work.

Creative layering

In this chapter I am going to cover some strange yet creative layering techniques which can be used more for effect than for single shot drum use. By this I mean that these techniques will help to add special efx or simply strange textures to existing productions.

Layering a single shot kick

The first example I am going to cover is one that entails layering a single shot drum hit, in this case a kick, and then layering that with another kick that has undergone left to right panning. Figure 11.1 displays a standard 808 kick tone.

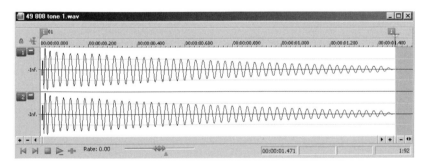

Figure 11.1
Standard 808 kick tone

Sound file

49 808 tone 1.wav

What I am going to do now is to create a pan effect that pans the kick tone from right to left. To do this I am going to use one of Sound Forge's generic tools: Menu/Process Pan/Expand (Figure 11.2).

The nodes in the Pan/Expand tool are used to create a pan envelope. You can create or delete as many nodes as required. Basically the location of the nodes determines the fade from either side of the stereo field to the opposing side. By creating an envelope curve that controls left/right fades one is able to hone the curve into a shape that is unique. I like this tool because of the huge amount of flexibility it affords to the user. For sounds that fade towards the tail end of the waveform one needs to consider compensating the gains so as to balance the stereo field pan. This is exactly what I have done with the envelope shape. Once rendered the waveform is shown in Figure 11.3.

Figure 11.2
The Pan/Expand tool

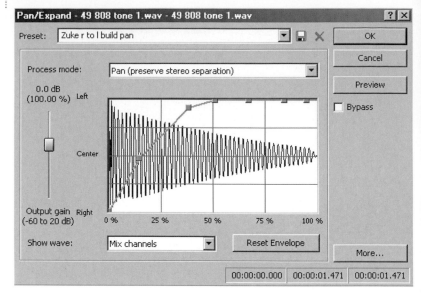

Sound file

49 808 tone 1 pan render.wav

Figure 11.3 shows the rendered waveform. The pan is clearly heard from right to left. You will notice how I have compensated for the fade and gain values so as to create a balanced pan movement.

Figure 11.3
The rendered waveform

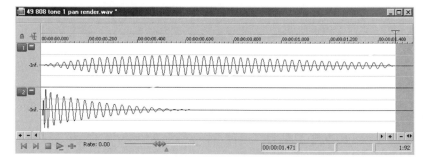

The next step is to find a suitable kick waveform and to layer the panned waveform with the 'dry' kick waveform to create a new sonic texture. Figure 11.4 shows the dry kick waveform.

Figure 11.4
The dry kick waveform

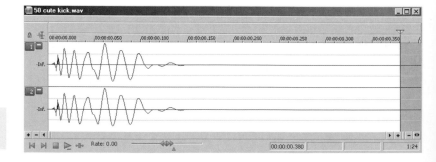

Sound file

50 cute kick.wav

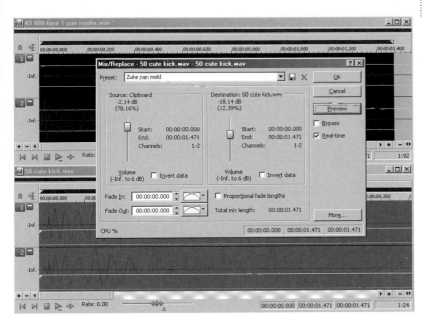

Figure 11.5
The mix process

Sound file

51 layered pan mix.wav

Now we can layer the two waveforms using the Paste / Special / Mix tool. Please make sure to adjust the gains to create the right level balance for the mix.

Figure 11.5 shows the mix process. Note that the dry layer is used gently with little gain. I have done this so as to shape the panned layer to have a little attack element but not too much so as to deter it from being an effect. Of course, you can mix to taste to create whatever resultant layer you want.

The slap back effect

The next example adopts a basic and simple technique that results in a sound having a slap back type of tail. Figure 11.6 shows a standard clap. By copying this waveform and then reversing it using the menu option 'Process / Reverse' we can layer the two to create the slap back effect.

Figure 11.6
A standard clap

Sound file

51 clap clipped.wav

Figure 11.7 displays the reversed waveform, and Figure 11.8 the mix settings.

Figure 11.7
The reversed waveform

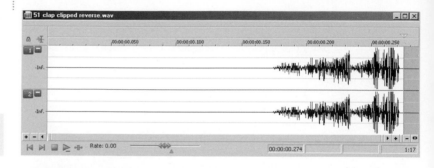

Figure 11.8
The mix settings

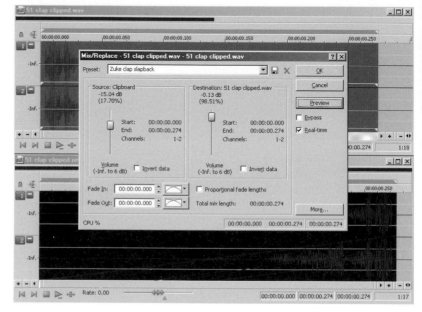

Delay pan in stereo

In the next example I am going to create a delay pan in stereo for a clap waveform and layer it with the original dry version. The important thing to note with time domain changes like delays is that file lengths vary and therefore must be matched when layering. Figure 11.9 displays the clap waveform. Figure 11.10 displays the delay effect and settings selected from the Sound Forge menu.

Figure 11.11 displays the rendered clap delay file and Figure 11.12 displays the mix function.

Figure 11.9
The clap waveform

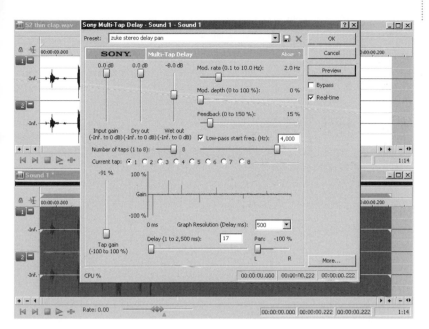

Figure 11.10
Delay effect and settings

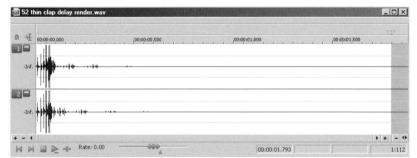

Figure 11.11
The rendered clap delay file

Sound file

52 thin clap delay render.wav

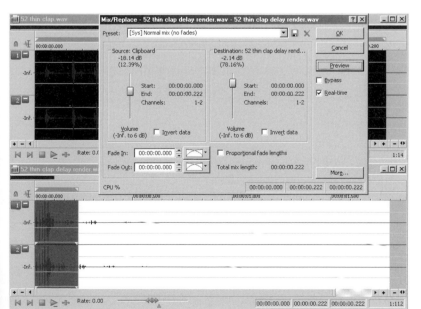

Figure 11.12
The mix function

Figure 11.13
The waveform length differences

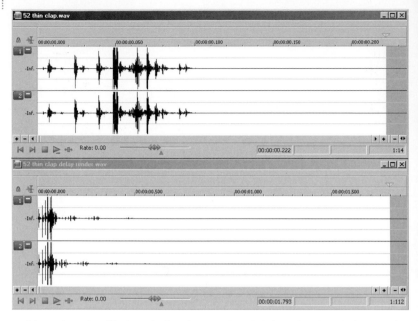

Figure 11.13
The waveform length differences

Note that the file length for the rendered delay clap in relation to the length of the dry original file. The highlighted area of the rendered file is equated to the waveform length of the original file.

If I were to select both waveforms and put one under the other, you could then see that the waveform lengths are very different because the delay process is time domain based and alters the waveform length. Figure 11.13 displays the waveform length differences.

However, I am going to copy both together without the waveform length equating so that I can then truncate and fade out the resultant waveform to my taste. I wanted to show you what a difference a time based effect can make to the overall waveform length and how it is important to take this process and its result into account when layering. Figure 11.14 shows the rendered mixed files after truncation and fade out.

Figure 11.14
The rendered mixed files after truncation and fade out

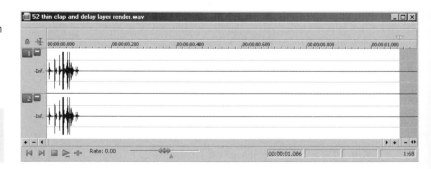

Sound file

52 thin clap and delay layer render.wav

Adding a slap back to a snare

In the next example I am going to add a slap back to a snare but using a different process to the one covered earlier. This is a good technique for adding a nice short repeat tail to a snare sound. Figure 11.15 shows the snare waveform.

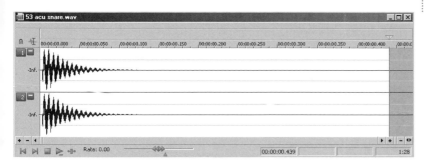

Figure 11.15
The snare waveform

Sound file

53 acu snare.wav

The effect I am going to apply to the copied waveform is called Gapper and is in the menu option Effects (Figure 11.16).

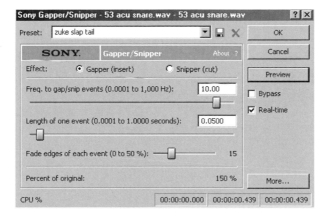

Figure 11.16
The Gapper effect and its settings

Sound file

53 acu snare Gapper rendered

Next, I am going to mix the two together making sure to allow for the gain variances and waveform lengths (Figure 11.17).

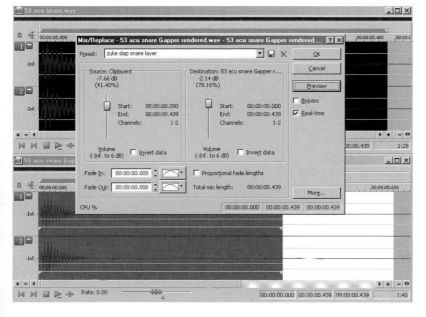

Figure 11.17
The mix process

Sound file

53 acu snare Gapper and dry rendered.wav

How to get a really deep kick sound

The next example is one of the simplest ways to attain a really deep kick sound without having to use extremes of EQ. It is a simple form of pitch shifting and layering. Figure 11.18 shows a simple mid hard hitting kick.

Figure 11.18
A simple mid hard hitting kick.

Sound file

54 underwater kick.wav

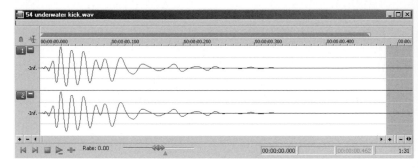

Once a clone of the file has been made, a simple form of pitch shifting takes place (Figure 11.19). And now the two layers are mixed together.

Figure 11.19
The pitch shifter and its settings

Sound file

54 underwater kick pitch shifted.wav

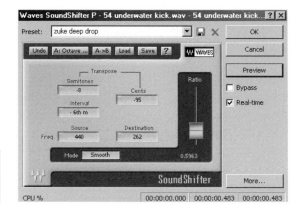

Figure 11.20 displays the resultant layer.

Figure 11.20
The resultant layer

Sound file

54 underwater kick pitch shifted res.wav

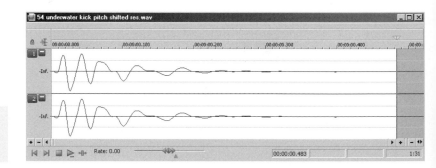

And just to give it some more gain in the body of the kick a compressor comes in handy. Figure 11.21 displays the compressor and its settings.

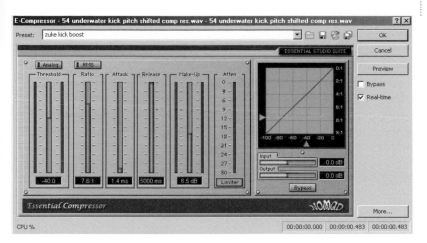

Figure 11.21
The compressor and its settings

Sound file

54 underwater kick pitch shifted
comp res.wav

Using a filter to treat the cloned layer

In the next example I am going to use a filter to treat the cloned layer of a nice and dirty snare sound. Figure 11.22 shows the snare waveform.

Figure 11.22
The snare waveform

Sound file

55 squelched snare.wav

Figure 11.23 displays the filter and its settings.

Figure 11.23
The filter settings

Sound file

55 squelched snare filtered.wav

And now the two waveforms (dry original and wet clone) will be layered to create the resultant layer.

Add a wah wah effect

I would like to end with a simple example using a wah-wah effect on the cloned layer and then mixing the dry and wet waveforms together to give a squelchy colour to the resultant layer. Figure 11.24 shows the grime snare waveform and Figure 11.25 displays the wah-wah and its settings. The dry and wet layers are mixed to create the resultant layer.

Figure 11.24
Grime snare waveform

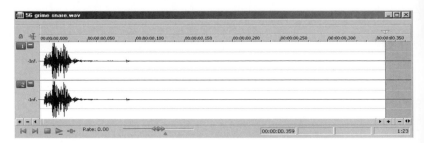

Figure 11.25
The wah-wah and its settings

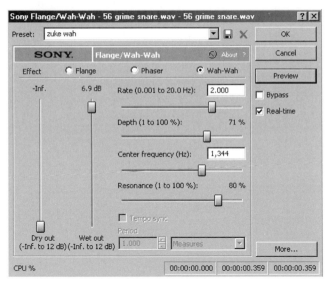

The examples in this chapter are simple and yet creative. Both effects and dynamics have been used to shape new sonic textures. Even if an effect or dynamic seems like an inappropriate choice for layering drum sounds there is nothing to stop you using them.

The beauty of the layering process is that you are not bound to predetermined ideas about what is right or wrong. The physics and maths are crucial but the design and result is purely down to your imagination.

I have only scratched the surface in terms of what can be achieved with the tools available today. Layering drum sounds is an art but there is science behind it as well. The marriage between the two will afford you the optimum results. Do not disregard either.

The last word

In this book I have tried to explain as clearly as possible the art and science of drum layering using the techniques I have learnt over the years as a producer and sound designer. These techniques are not exclusive to me, far from it; they have been used by countless producers for many years.

The advent of both the computer and the relevant software has made these techniques available to all. It was not that long ago that the only tools available to us were tape, a razor blade, a hardware sampler (if you were rich and lucky), patience and a great deal of imagination. Today we are spoilt for choice, both in terms of hardware and software, and I believe this is what has made the learning processes very daunting, confusing and simply time consuming. It is always refreshing to go back to basics and to simplify the whole learning curve. I hope I have achieved this with this book.

My final, and only, advice to you is to master the theory, practice the techniques and most important of all; enjoy yourself. Who knows? Maybe I will be buying your book in the future.

Thank you for purchasing this book and taking this journey with me.

Eddie Bazil
www.samplecraze.com

Index